A Complete Guide to Learning Contracts

A Complete
Guide to

Learning
Contracts

George Boak

Gower

Published by
Gower Publishing Limited
Gower House
Croft Road
Aldershot
Hampshire GU11 3HR
England

Gower
Old Post Road
Brookfield
Vermont 05036
USA

George Boak has asserted his right under the Copyright, Designs and Patents Act 1988 to be identified as the author of this work.

British Library Cataloguing in Publication Data
Boak, George
   A complete guide to learning contracts
   1. Education – Aims and objectives 2. Contracts – Great Britain
   I. Title
   370.1'1

ISBN 0 566 07927 5

2418870 0

Library of Congress Cataloging-in-Publication Data

Boak, George, 1953–
   A complete guide to learning contracts / George Boak.
        p.   cm.
   Includes bibliographical references (p.   ) and index.
   ISBN 0–566–07927–5 (hardcover)
   1. Learning contracts.   I.Title.
LB1029.L43B63   1998
371.39—DC21   97–20723
                                                                CIP

Phototypeset in Palatino by Intype London Ltd and printed in Great Britain by Hartnolls Ltd, Bodmin.

Contents

List of figures and tables   vii
Preface   ix

 1 Introducing learning contracts   1
 2 Learning contracts, skills and competences   13
 3 Design and development   29
 4 Priming   43
 5 Learning needs analysis   53
 6 First steps in negotiation   67
 7 Advanced negotiation   83
 8 Agreeing assessment measures   97
 9 Negotiation skills   111
10 Support   125
11 Assessment   139
12 Three-way contracts   153

References   167
Index   171

List of figures and tables

Figures

2.1 The learning triangle   14
2.2 Sources of learning about job-related skills   16
2.3 The Learning Cycle   19
2.4 Staged improvement   22
2.5 Stages in competence development   26
3.1 Example of a simple learning contract form   32
3.2 Activities involved in delivering the contract   34
3.3 A simple design   36
3.4 A management development programme   36
3.5 A learning contract as part of a longer programme of study   37
3.6 A postgraduate diploma   38
3.7 Multiple learning contracts   40
5.1 Using different models at different stages   57
6.1 Contributing to the contract   68
8.1 The Learning Cycle   102
9.1 Overlapping objectives (based on Kennedy *et al.* 1984)   112
10.1 Double loop learning   136
11.1 Trade-offs between growth in practical ability and growth in theoretical understanding   145
12.1 The extended learning triangle   162

Tables

10.1 Research activities and possible support   127
10.2 Skills development activities and possible support   128

Preface

Learning contracts are formal agreements between a learner and someone who is helping them to learn. They are a popular and valuable component of self-managed learning, and they can provide an effective supportive structure for individualized learning and assessment in a wide range of diverse circumstances. They are currently being used on a range of educational and training programmes, from postgraduate degrees to simple programmes of self-development. While they are particularly useful for work-based learning and for the development of skills and competences, they are also of value in structuring research projects or agreeing individualized portfolios of traditional academic study.

This book is written for users of learning contracts of all levels of experience – from novices to seasoned practitioners. It is for the tutors, trainers, coaches or mentors who will negotiate contracts with learners, support them, and ultimately assess them. Its aim is to help tutors and trainers, and learners, to devise better, more effective, more worthwhile learning contracts.

The advice in this book is based on twelve years' experience of using learning contracts with managers in a variety of situations, and also on interested observation of the use of contracts by others. In parts this book is an update and revision of *Developing Managerial Competence: the Management Learning Contract Approach*, which was published in 1991. Those who bought and used that book will find much that is new in this one. Learning contracts have become much more popular in the intervening years, and there have been significant developments in their application.

The book follows the cycle of the contracting process, from the design of the programme through to the assessment of the contract. After the first chapter, which sets out a basic definition of terms, it is designed to be dipped into, consulted as appropriate, used as required.

It would not have been possible to write this book without the help, insight and support of a great many people – colleagues who worked on learning contracts with me, clients whose enthusiastic support ensured the widespread use of contracts, trainers and tutors in other organizations whose work provided further insight and comparisons, and writers on aspects of personal learning and development who laid the foundations for the approach.

Most of all it would not have been worthwhile without the efforts of the hundreds of learners who, with courage and honesty, exercised the choices and undertook the risks of contract learning. There are numerous real-life examples of their efforts in the text – only the names have been changed, to protect the innocent. To those who took to contract learning with energy and enthusiasm, to those who embraced its freedoms and responsibilities only reluctantly, and to those who challenged in a dozen different ways its strengths and limitations – thank you.

George Boak
October 1997

Chapter 1

Introducing learning contracts

The term 'learning contract' has become increasingly popular in education and training circles over the past ten years. The price of popularity has been an increasing slackness of definition, so that the description is applied in a variety of contexts to refer to a family of related but slightly different learning methods.

The growth in popularity of learning contracts is due to a recognition of their effectiveness in supporting flexible, individualized programmes of learning. All learning contracts, however loosely the term is applied, share certain characteristics: a degree of choice for the learner, a learning plan, and (usually) an agreement between the learner and someone who will help them – a tutor, trainer, coach or mentor.

Experience shows that effective learning contracts incorporate additional features: they are formal, written agreements, and they set out clearly what will be learned, how the learning will be achieved, and how it will be evaluated. They provide a wide range of choice, which enhances the learner's motivation and commitment. They are supported, monitored and assessed.

In this introductory chapter we explore some of the key characteristics of effective learning contracts, see how they may be used in different situations and with different subject matter, and summarize the benefits of the contract approach to learning.

What is a learning contract?

We define an effective learning contract as:

a formal, written agreement between a learner and a tutor (or a trainer, or a coach) about what the learner will learn and how that learning will be measured.

This section briefly reviews some of the differences between learning contracts, and attempts to answer some of the most common initial questions about contract learning.

Long and short contracts

One of the main differences in the use of the term 'learning contract' is a matter of scale.

Sometimes the choices a student makes at the outset of a course of study, which identify the range of topics and options and learning goals that will be undertaken over the next twelve months, are described as a 'learning contract'. This learning plan, agreed between the student and the college, is typically made up of choices from a menu of alternatives, and contains a number of quite different goals and aims, with little detail about how these will be achieved.

This book is concerned with a type of agreement which is more creative and operational. It concentrates on a particular area of knowledge and/or skill. In addition to specifying learning objectives, it usually includes some points about the learner's plan of action and about how the contract will be assessed. Often – although not always – it will be shorter in duration than the student's main choice of syllabus.

These learning contracts can be used in a wide variety of situations, from inclusion in university degree courses, to deployment in the development of job-specific skills through personal development plans and secondments.

Written agreements

Must learning contracts always be in writing? Experience shows that in order to be effective, learning contracts must always have a written component. The contract will contain details of learning objectives, a plan of action and assessment measures, and for the sake of clarity and shared understanding, even the simplest contract needs to be expressed in some durable form. The written words may not always encompass every detail of the agreement, but they should capture the key points.

Who makes the contract?

Learning contracts are generally agreed between a learner and a person who will help them to learn, who may be a professional educator or trainer, or a colleague or friend with an interest in the learner's development, or their immediate line manager. As learning contracts are used in a wide variety of situations, the title used for this person may be a tutor, a trainer, a coach, a mentor, an adviser, a learning facilitator, etc. Throughout this book the word *tutor* will be used, simply to avoid constant repetition of this string of alternatives. For the same reasons of simplicity we shall talk of *learners*, rather than students, participants, candidates, etc.

Sometimes it is asked whether this second person is necessary: can I, the learner, not make a contract with myself? This appears to me to be stretching the use of the word: a person may establish a *plan* by themselves, but a contract requires some agreement: do we talk of a person *agreeing* with themselves? Whether the use of the word 'contract' will stretch this far or not, effective learning contracts need at least two parties to the agreement.

In some cases there will be more than two parties. Contracts for work-based learning often seek to involve the learner's line manager, or a mentor in addition to the contract tutor, and the agreement becomes three-sided.

Is a learning contract legally binding?

The use of the word 'contract' sometimes gives rise to apprehensions based on its associations.

Clark (1996) says 'The learning contract is not a legally binding document, but the metaphor of a contract is used to allude to the serious commitment participants will make' to working towards the goals specified in the agreement. This is the essence of the case. However, the terms of a learning contract might feature in an appeal against an assessment by a disgruntled student, so there is arguably a sense in which the terms have legal force.

There are sometimes apprehensions about the use of the word 'contract' in certain contexts. It was considered to be a word that would give rise to negative associations in the health service, when 'contracting out' meant threats to jobs. In another context, one particular organization felt that 'learning contracts' were associated with developing junior staff and trainees, and more senior staff should be offered the chance to use 'negotiated learning agreements'. Which had all the characteristics of what, in this book, we are calling learning contracts.

Contracts and assessment

There are different views on the importance of assessment in learning contracts.

In some learning programmes, contracts are agreed but are not assessed. The proponents of this approach generally recognize the benefits of assessment, but argue that an action planning and contracting approach can be of value to the individual without necessarily involving assessment by another person (Powers 1987).

On the other hand, there are strong arguments to suggest that assessment is fundamental to the whole contract process.

- The precision of the targets enhances the learner's motivation.
- The involvement of another person in assessing the learning contract at a specified time enhances motivation and the accuracy of the evaluation.
- Assessing progress against the agreed measures is a means of evaluating whether the learning contract has been effective or not.

The learning in the 'learning contract'

In recent years some tutors have become very familiar with the process of making written agreements about assessment with learners. This has been in the context of National Vocational Qualifications and Scottish Vocational Qualifications (NVQs and SVQs) where tutors and learners often reach specific agreements on what will count as evidence of a certain level of skill or competence. The learner then goes ahead and gathers the evidence. There may be some learning involved, there may not. These agreements are sometimes called learning contracts, although their main aim is often not learning but the collection of evidence.

Effective learning contracts, which have as their main aim the development of the learner's knowledge and/or skill, add more value and generally gain more commitment from the learner than contracts which do not involve learning. The test is not the context – effective learning contracts are used on some NVQ and SVQ programmes – but whether the aim of the contract is to increase the learner's knowledge or skills.

Benefits of learning contracts

Effective learning contracts possess two principal characteristics, flexibility and focus, from which flow a number of benefits.

- *Flexibility*: The contract approach allows choice and variation in what is learned, to suit the learner's wants and needs. Learning contracts can be used to address any learning area. Within a particular training or development programme the scope may be more limited, but it should still be more wide-ranging than any choice of pre-packaged options.

- *Focus*: From the range of choices and variations available, an effective learning contract helps the learner to focus attention on specific objectives, outcomes and actions. The formal nature of a written agreement provides a firm structure to guide and support each individual contract.

Both characteristics are desirable for an effective contract. Without flexibility, most of the benefits of using learning contracts are lost. Without focus, learners can easily lose their way.

The benefits that derive from these characteristics are as follows:

1. Learning can be more relevant. The goals of a contract can be matched to the learner's needs and to the opportunities in the learner's situation. This is particularly useful for work-based learning, where the circumstances of individual learners differ. Learning contracts can help learners take deliberate action to develop skills relevant to their circumstances (Mumford 1993).

2. Learners can play a leading role in designing the contract – particularly in identifying the goals they wish to achieve. Learning contracts can provide an escape from prescriptive learning, or from a choice between bundles of items on a menu of options.

3. It follows that learning contracts are generally motivational. They usually generate more enthusiasm and a more lasting effect than those learning experiences that have been designed by tutors or trainers. As well as the effects of responsibility and relevance, the clarity of the agreement also has a positive effect on motivation: this requires clear objectives, action plans and assessment measures.

4. Learning contracts provide a mechanism for focusing support and resources on a learner's needs. A detailed discussion of learning objectives and an action plan for achieving them will naturally cover the resources which are needed for success. Such a discussion will not magically create resources where none previously existed, but it can cause all who are involved in the contract – the learner, the tutor, the company, the educational institution – to consider how best to use existing resources, and how best to expand them in the future.

5. Learning contracts can provide a means of accrediting a wide range of relevant learning. They can be incorporated into programmes leading to qualifications, and thereby import the benefits of increased relevance, responsibility and increased motivation into these programmes. The qualification also often improves the learner's motivation.

6. Successful learning contracts can help individuals to develop skills of independent learning and thereby help them to continue learning beyond the end of the particular programme. This enhances their ability to manage changing situations and changing needs in the future.

Of course, these are no more than *potential* benefits. They are not guaranteed with every use of a learning contract. Much depends on the skills and the attitudes of the parties to the agreement.

The learner must be prepared to learn, must be willing to take the initiative in proposing the terms of the contract, and must be prepared to see it through.

Tutors may need to change their normal approach to learners. They must be prepared to listen, to question, to summarize and to support. They may

---

Box 1.1 Principles of adult learning

Malcolm Knowles (1986) argues that learning contracts relate to basic principles of adult learning, in particular:

1. Adults are generally able and willing to take responsibility for their own learning.
2. Individuals bring a variety of experiences to learning, which can be pooled to form a rich resource.
3. Adults are most ready to learn when they can see the relevance to their own needs and wants.
4. Individuals have their own unique styles and paces of learning, and a unique pattern of outside commitments and pressures, goals and motivations.

Wherever these principles apply, learning contracts may be appropriate. Knowles also notes that people used to more traditional methods of learning may need to be reorientated towards the contract approach, and that contract learning may pose particular problems for learners with a high dependency on direction from others.

---

also be responsible for designing, organizing and introducing the contract approach, and enlisting support from others.

There may be other parties to the contract. Where contracts are used as part of work-based learning, their success will be more likely if the learner's employer – represented by their immediate boss or department head – is prepared to provide some support, too.

Learning contracts and qualifications

In the UK there have been pressures in recent years to increase the flexibility and the vocational relevance of qualifications courses.

In the USA, where learning contracts have been used for several years in some institutions as part of degree programmes, most contracts are concerned with the specific subject area the student will research, the resources to be used and the nature of the paper that will be written to show understanding. Many of these contracts involve acquiring and using knowledge and, in the course of this, demonstrating conceptual skills (Knowles 1986; Hall and Kevles 1982; on the UK experience see Laycock and Stephenson 1993).

Theoretically, it is possible for a qualification programme to consist entirely of learning contracts – this may be a reasonable way to structure a higher degree attained by research, but in practice most qualification programmes afford less scope for contract learning. All learning contracts on qualification courses operate within some constraints, usually concerning the broad area that is covered and the level of achievement shown in the assessment.

Perhaps the main reason is that most qualifications are subject to an implicit assumption that part of the programme of study concerns some common core of knowledge and skills. There may be additional options or electives, but all students who follow the programme are expected to cover the core. With professional qualifications, for example, doctors, surveyors, accountants, lawyers may specialize in some areas of their profession, at their choice, but all are expected to be competent in certain common areas. This limits the scope for the effective use of learning contracts, which are most valuable when they are used to structure different individual learning experiences. However, they may still be used in these circumstances – as part of options, or even as elective components of core modules of the qualification.

Consider an extreme case: in a core module, early in an undergraduate degree programme, the range of choices available to a learner is likely to be very limited, and the learner's level of understanding – which is the basis on which he/she can make informed choices – may be slight. It may be more cost-effective to structure the learning by more standardized, less individualized means: common texts, common tasks, group delivery (seminar/lecture/tutorial) and common assignments or reports. Later in the programme there may be more scope for individual choice, both in terms of the constraints of the syllabus and the learner's level of understanding.

An issue which is sometimes raised where learning contracts are proposed as part of a programme that leads to a qualification concerns the application of common standards. The contracts carried out by one learner should be of equal weight to the contracts carried out by another. How can this be achieved if the contracts are about very different subjects?

In fact there are precedents for the inclusion of learning contracts in such programmes. Most certificates, diplomas and degrees have for many years included dissertations or 'projects' – individual pieces of research work, the aims and scope of which have been negotiated by learner and tutor.

Are there differences between learning contracts and these 'projects'?

In practice there may not be any difference. The agreement between the learner and the project supervisor might meet our basic criteria for an effective learning contract, i.e. that it is a *formal, written agreement about what the learner will learn and how that learning will be measured*. Incorporating a learning contract into the process of agreeing projects or dissertations will generally improve the quality of learning. However, the arrangements for undertaking a project or dissertation do not always include such a formal agreement.

Box 1.2 Contracts, qualifications and constraints

Where learning contracts are part of a programme leading to a qualification there will probably be constraints in the following areas.

- *The broad subject matter they cover*: if a contract is included within a specialist area, then the learner may need to choose from the possibilities within that area; e.g. Housing Policy, Education Practice, Financial Management, Strategic Analysis.

- *The content of assessment*: there may be an expectation that learners will be able to relate their chosen contract area to a recognized body of knowledge that is relevant to the particular qualification; in this sense learners do not have a free choice about some areas of study and assessment. This is likely to be more of a constraint in higher-degree programmes and programmes which have a strong core identity, such as some professional qualifications.

- *The form of assessment*: for example, one postgraduate degree programme that uses learning contracts requires that all assessment takes the form of reports written by the learner – because this is part of postgraduate degree policy for the university; some parity is sought between the length of the reports on this programme and those produced for other programmes.

Work-based learning

Learning contracts are particularly suitable for work-based learning: indeed, their increased popularity in the UK in recent times owes much to a growing emphasis on various forms of learning in the workplace.

Part of this has been brought about by the need for organizations to cope with the increasing speed of change. The literature on the 'learning organization' has grown, and the launch of 'lifelong learning' initiatives (for example, DfEE 1995 and 1996) signify the need for continuous development of knowledge and skills. At the same time, providers of education have been encouraged to be more closely orientated towards the needs of employers, the world of work and work-based learning (Mansfield and Mitchell 1996; DfEE 1995 and 1996; Council for Industry and Higher Education 1995; SCALE 1992; Employment Department 1989/90).

There are a number of different types of individual agreements which support work-based learning. In some cases they are called 'learning con-

---

Box 1.3 The learning organization

The idea of organizational learning appears to have originated with Argyris and Schon (1978).

The learning organization has been defined as 'an organization which facilitates the learning of all of its members and continuously transforms itself' (Pedler *et al.* 1991).

It has been seen as an organization where training and personal development are an integral part of daily activities, and where learning is a continuous process, closely related to actions in the workplace, rather than an activity performed intermittently with the help of the training department or external courses (Barham *et al.* 1988).

Jones and Hendry (1992) summarize the ideas of a range of commentators, indicating degrees of consensus in defining what remains a broad concept. A major contribution has been made by Peter Senge's ideas (1991) on the disciplines that are needed to create learning organizations.

---

tracts', in other situations they go by other names. Current common types include the following.

1. Personal development plans (PDPs) which are part of an organization's appraisal and development system. In their simplest form, they may be agreed between an employee and his/her immediate boss, and their targets are noted as part of the overall system. They are a form of learning contract – although they may be large in scale, and contain a number of disparate goals, with little detail about action plans or methods of assessment. Some may be expressed in the shorthand of inputs, or 'experience', rather than clear learning objectives.

    PDPs or learning contracts may be negotiated between the learner and the training department within the organization in a number of different circumstances. The employee's immediate boss may be drawn into agreeing, supporting and assessing the contract.

2. An individual contract approach is often used in large organizations when the employees in question are identified as trainees, or people with high potential, and the training department has a brief to develop them through (among other means) various kinds of work experience. As in the case of PDPs agreed with the line manager, the contracts may be of the larger-scale, over-arching type, covering a number of different goals over a period of time.

3. Training departments may also use individual learning contracts or 'action plans' as extensions of training programmes which have already included off-the-job events, to encourage transfer of learning to the

workplace. Usually in these cases the people who have attended the training course are encouraged to devise their action plan and discuss it with their colleagues, and the economics of the training programme may prohibit detailed discussion between a trainer and individual learners to devise or to assess the action plan. In training programmes that use action learning sets, the group meets at regular intervals and the individual members report back to their colleagues on progress – more on this in Chapter 2.

4.   In some large organizations, training departments design and run programmes that lead to qualifications, and they may use learning contracts as part of these programmes. These learning contracts will be individually negotiated and assessed.

In some cases, part of the function of a training department is undertaken by an agency external to the organization – a college, a university or a training organization. This agency may deliver training programmes for the organization, such as those in point 3 above. They may also provide a variety of qualification programmes which include some work-based learning.

5.   Applied Certificate, Diploma or Master's programmes may attract individual employees of the organization, and may include some attendance at seminars or workshops off the job and some demonstration of work-related ability. At certificate or diploma levels these may be related to occupational standards, and lead to National Vocational Qualifications, which focus on performance in the workplace.

6.   Situations where the learner is on temporary placement within the organization – typically as part of an undergraduate degree programme – and the learning contract is designed to structure the learning that is the primary purpose of the period of work experience.

In some of these cases, the agreements which are reached would satisfy our definition of a learning contract: they would be written agreements setting out what the learner will learn and how that learning will be measured. In some cases the agreements would be looser or larger or less formal.

Organizations sometimes arrange for staff to take responsibility for change projects, as part of their development. This might apply in any of the situations set out above, perhaps particularly in 1, 2 and 6.

Is there a difference between undertaking a learning contract and managing a change project for developmental reasons? Superficially the experiences may appear the same – and may in fact be used in conjunction with one another. However, there are usually differences in the objectives in each case.

In a learning contract, the objectives concern what the individual will learn, and the evaluation or assessment concerns the learning. In a change project there are objectives that concern the accomplishment of the task, which will often take precedence over an explicit focus on learning. We shall return to this distinction in the following chapter.

Although learning contracts are very suitable for work-based learning, their application is by no means problem-free. A common difficulty is how to accommodate changes in the learner's circumstances.

Learning contracts are perhaps the best mechanism for accommodating differences in learners' needs, interests and situations. Work-based learning contracts can be designed to take advantage of specific circumstances in the learner's working life. However, work environments can change in unpredictable ways, leading to rapid changes in needs and priorities. This is a particular threat to contracts that are expected to cover a long period of time (such as a year). It is also a threat to contracts that are expected to cover new jobs, including secondments – which are perhaps more subject to change than established positions.

With the increased range of variation in work-based learning contracts, the role of the tutor can become more complex. The learner's choice of contract area may stretch into places beyond the experience or expertise of the tutor: especially where the learner is making judgements about aspects of his/her individual work environment. This limits the ability of the tutor to provide realistic advice when negotiating the contract, to provide ongoing support in the course of the contract, and to apply realistic assessment measures at the contract's conclusion.

It is worth braving these difficulties, however, and seeking intelligent solutions to these problems, for the benefits of using work-based learning contracts easily outweigh the costs.

Review

In this chapter learning contracts have been introduced as

formal agreements between a learner and a tutor about what the learner will learn and how that learning will be measured.

The principal characteristics and benefits of learning contracts have been discussed, and we have seen that contracts may be used in a variety of situations. Their use in courses leading to qualifications and in work-based learning programmes has been considered.

The next chapter concerns the use of learning contracts to develop skills and competences. This is a common aim of contracts used in work-based learning. Contracts of this type can be a little more complicated than contracts that simply aim to improve a person's knowledge and understanding.

Chapter 2

Learning contracts, skills and competences

Learning contracts provide a valuable means of helping learners to develop relevant skills and competences.

The previous chapter commented on the growing concern in recent times with continuous development of work-related knowledge and skills, which has led to renewed interest in methods of encouraging and supporting work-based learning. The priority of most work-based learning is the development of relevant skills and competences. To know, to understand, is seldom sufficient: the learner needs to learn how to behave in different ways in order to meet the new challenges of the changing world.

The concern with work-related skills has been expressed in the development of a number of systematic models of the competences (or competencies) which are thought to be required for effective performance in various job roles. In the UK and Australia, national competence models have been developed for specific occupations; in those countries and in the USA and Canada, numerous in-company competence models have also been designed, which have been exported world-wide by their use in multinational companies.

Learning contracts provide a particularly suitable framework for the development of skills and competences in the workplace. Learning contracts can be individualized to match particular needs and particular situations, and they can provide a supportive structure for a person who needs to develop in a certain area.

Learning contracts can also bring together the three partners in the triangle of work-related learning: the tutor, the learner and the representative of the employer – the learner's line manager (Figure 2.1). This is often a relationship characterized by lack of communication, and conflict.

The breakdown in communication in traditional education, training and development tends to be between the tutor and the line manager, giving rise to a lack of understanding and sometimes antagonism. Line managers (and sometimes learners) often complain about the lack of relevance of the training and the insularity of the tutors, while tutors complain about

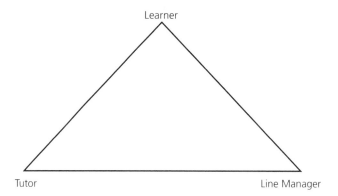

Figure 2.1   The learning triangle

the poor motivation and negative attitudes of the line manager (and sometimes of the learners).

Learners can suffer through the ignorance of tutors and the doubts which line managers cast on the value of the training programme.

While learning contracts do not resolve all of the underlying tensions between the different aims and interests of the three parties, they at least provide a way of bringing them together in an open discussion of the priorities for learning and development. One senior Training and Development Manager from British Gas, now retired, was fond of saying that this results in two people being trained for the price of one.

There are, however, certain issues to be addressed when using learning contracts for these purposes, and certain models and approaches which appear to be more effective than others. These are the subjects of this chapter.

Developing skills

If the acquisition of knowledge and the development of understanding represent one dimension of learning, the development of skills represents another. Each of us develops ranges of skills throughout our lives, including simple psycho-motor skills, personal organizational skills, social skills, conceptual skills, and skills relating specifically to our occupation, family roles, hobbies and interests. For most of us, development is not constant throughout our lives. There are periods of improvement and there are plateaux, and sometimes periods of decline. There may be periods when we take deliberate steps to improve on a particular skill, and times when we are able to improve by fortuitous circumstance. Learning may be difficult or easy. For some skills we may seem to have a natural predisposition, for others there appear to be natural limits.

Box 2.1 Contracts, skills and competences: the experience

Between 1986 and 1995, together with a small number of colleagues at the Northern Regional Management Centre (NRMC) in Washington, UK, I negotiated and assessed learning contracts with people working in a wide range of diverse organizations – including local authorities and petro-chemical companies, mass manufacturers and retailers, project engineers, finance companies, fire brigades and police forces.

Most of the work took place in the context of accredited programmes that would lead to qualifications, but the emphasis within the contracts was primarily on the development of practical management skills in the workplace. To emphasize the skills orientation of these contracts, we called them Management Learning Contracts (MLCs) (Boak and Stephenson 1987; Boak 1991a).

One programme led to a Certificate in Management Studies. The learners were either junior managers, or aspiring to management positions.

From 1989, a combined Diploma and MBA programme was provided by a group of staff drawn from four higher education institutes in the region, co-ordinated by NRMC consultants, using learning contracts linked to a model of management competences. The learners included senior and middle managers from a variety of public and private sector organizations (Boak 1991b; Pascoe 1992).

Thompson's research (1994) indicates that managers who used learning contracts on these programmes felt that they experienced significant learning and growth. General high-growth areas were identified as increased self-confidence and self-management, and a better ability to handle uncertainties and new situations.

Programmes leading to National Vocational Qualifications in Management were also delivered, from 1992.

In the process of delivering these programmes a great deal was learned about the contract approach to developing skills and competences.

These programmes are still successfully operating from Newcastle Business School, in the University of Northumbria at Newcastle.

The development of many practical and occupational skills is often attributed to learning from experience. Building on the work-based learning ideas of Levy, for example, Gattegno identifies four sources of individual learning about job-related skills (Figure 2.2) – education, training and development, a challenging work role and lessons learned from key work relationships (Levy 1991; Gattegno 1995). McCall and colleagues at the Center for Creative Leadership have focused on the value of experiential learning, and particularly the developmental value of challenging jobs

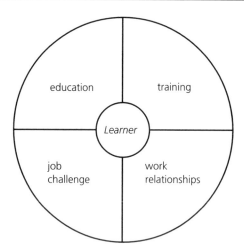

Figure 2.2   Sources of learning about job-related skills

(McCall *et al.* 1988). Revans developed the action learning approach on the basis of a profound distrust of the academic profession, and the belief that people learn best when they are able to reflect upon their own efforts to tackle difficult problems in the workplace (Revans 1980).

It is evident, however, that some individuals can undergo challenging experiences without learning much – or anything – from them. This may be for three prime reasons.

1.   They are too concerned with completing the task and meeting the immediate challenge, with very little effort left for learning.

Some learning may take place (depending on the task) but not as much as would occur if there was more emphasis on learning.

2.   They may be unaware of some or all of their own learning needs.

This is particularly true in the case of less obvious learning needs. For example, a person commencing a new project may be aware that they need to learn about the facts of the project and where it fits into the company, and about the other people who are working on the project, their names and their abilities. But they may be much less aware that – for example – they need to improve their influencing skills and their teambuilding skills if they are to be successful on this project. This may lead them to interpret events in ways that do not help them to learn (for example ascribing failures to bad luck or to the actions of others, rather than considering what they might have done differently).

3.   They may have undeveloped learning skills.

Even if they are aware of their own shortcomings, they may not know how to overcome them. We can help people to learn more effectively from experience by:

- making them more conscious of learning as an (important) activity
- helping them to determine their development needs
- helping them to understand the learning process and to develop their learning skills.

The intelligent use of learning contracts for skills development helps individuals in these ways. A complementary approach, to which contract learning owes a great deal, is action learning.

Action learning

Action learning was pioneered by Reg Revans from the 1950s onwards, as an approach to work-based learning, primarily for managers. There are varieties of approach to action learning (Pedler 1997; Lawrence 1994; see also Thompson and Stephenson 1991) but we can summarize the key features as:

- learners take responsibility for their own learning
- learners improve their job performance through action and through analysis of action in real and difficult work situations
- learners meet regularly in groups to discuss the plans, activities and progress of each member
- the group (or 'learning set') assist one another, through questioning and discussion, to tackle the work problems successfully and to achieve personal change and development in the process.

The learning contract approach to work-based learning has benefited from the insights of action learning. The emphasis on the development of practical knowledge and skills is common to both approaches, as is the emphasis on individual responsibility for learning and on action as a fundamental component of personal development. Action learning methods and learning contracts can be used together, to complement each other. But they are not identical approaches (despite some practitioners talking of a 'contract' between the individual and the group). The group support, questioning and discussion at the heart of the action learning approach is not necessary with learning contracts, nor is the practical work problem which the learner is attempting to resolve. Similarly, the formal, written agreement of the learning contract, with its explicit learning objectives, its action plan and assessment measures, is not central to action learning.

This is a significant difference. Learning contracts require each person to design his/her own programme of development and to be held responsible for it, whereas the group nature of action learning can diffuse individual

---

Box 2.2 The enjoyment factor

Thompson analysed 300 feedback reports from learners who completed the Certificate in Management Studies programme. There was general enthusiasm for the use of learning contracts. The most frequently cited reasons were:

- an almost unlimited choice of topics
- personal involvement in setting objectives, limits, deadlines, means and methods of learning to be undertaken, etc.
- personal responsibility for the overall learning
- self-assessment of personal/professional achievement
- a new challenge
- flexibility of topics/methods/assessment
- topics that were related to work demands, and therefore relevant.

Thompson 1994
See also Prideaux and Ford 1988; Garavan and Sweeney 1994

---

accountability. On the other hand, the interaction in an action learning set can be a rich source of development in itself, which a solitary individual undertaking a learning contract will not experience.

In either method, when people are engaged in developing their skills, it helps if they are made aware of learning processes, of the skills of learning, and of their own development needs. A useful model in this respect is the Learning Cycle.

The Learning Cycle

Since its development and promotion by David Kolb (1976) and Peter Honey and Alan Mumford (1982), the Cycle has been in widespread use on training and development programmes. The models are slightly different: here we shall use the Honey and Mumford terminology.

According to Honey and Mumford, people acquire skills by undertaking four different types of activity, represented on the Cycle as Action, Reflection, Knowledge, Planning (Figure 2.3).

Let us suppose that I am moving into a new post where much of my effectiveness will depend on my ability to work co-operatively with others and persuade them to work co-operatively with me. We can begin with ACTION – I make my first attempts to work with others and to convince them to co-operate with me. These attempts may be successful or may result in a degree of failure.

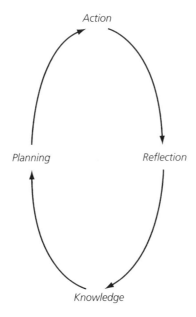

Figure 2.3   The Learning Cycle

If I am trying to develop my skill here, repeat my successes and avoid repeating my failures in the future, I should REFLECT on what has happened – what has happened? What did I do right? What did I do wrong? Depending on the complexity of the situation, issues of causality may not be at all clear; serious and instructive reflection may involve effort and insight.

Perhaps from this, some principles will emerge – the KNOWLEDGE stage of the Cycle. These may be general theories, they may be rules of thumb. They may be augmented by the advice of friends and colleagues, by books I seek out on co-operation, teamwork, persuasion, or information from lectures I attend. (Traditional education and training is often very strong on the knowledge component of skills.)

I then do some PLANNING for my next attempt to work with others, and I consider which of my general principles (or rules of thumb) are applicable to this instance, and how it should be approached.

I may go round the Cycle many times before I become truly skilled in this area.

The principles of the Learning Cycle embody important lessons for the construction of a learning contract to develop an individual's skills. The Cycle emphasizes that the development of skill is more than the acquisition of knowledge: some action should also be undertaken, and then evaluated.

The Cycle can be used to structure the contract:

- a specific skill area can be identified for development
- specific actions can be agreed with the learner, depending on his/her needs and the opportunities available
- a relevant supporting knowledge base can be identified, or the means of developing one can be built into the contract
- a structure for reflection on the experience, and for further action planning, can be agreed.

Using the Learning Cycle intelligently, the learner and the tutor can agree a series of activities that will lead to genuine development of skill and competence.

Targets for skills development

In setting out a learning contract, the specific skill the learner wants to develop must be targeted. Having a clear target is an important part of the supportive structure of the contract. This is often difficult – learners find it harder to speak the language of skills than the language of knowledge, and need assistance and support in defining their target skills, and in devising a suitable action plan and assessment measures. Part of this assistance may be in the nature of needs analysis to identify priority areas for development. Another part of it is in helping learners to understand how to define skills.

A useful approach to adopt in this context is to encourage learners to break skills into components. Most broad skill areas are amenable to further breakdown: this is the basis of most models of good practice. The process of identifying the components of the model of good practice may be something which is undertaken by the learner alone, or in a group, or with the help of a tutor, or with the help of published materials, models and ideas. The model of good practice can form a part of the learner's identification of their specific needs.

It is often helpful to encourage learners to think in terms of specific and generic skills. A specific skill is related to particular features of the learner's situation, whereas a generic skill is transferable across a range of situations. For example, the ability to understand my company's balance sheet is a specific skill, whereas the ability to understand balance sheets is a generic one. Similarly the ability to co-operate with my immediate colleagues is more specific than the ability to co-operate with people in general.

Learners' wants and needs often lie first and foremost in the development of skills to be used in specific situations – but the immediate expression of them may be as a generic skill. Identifying clear, realistic and beneficial targets may be a matter of helping the learner to express the skill in terms of the specific situation. If appropriate, some development of the generic skill can also be achieved by reference to the Learning Cycle structure – for example, by the learner:

> ## Box 2.3 What skills have been developed?
>
> An analysis of 950 learning contracts undertaken between 1986 and 1994 as part of the Certificate in Management Studies programme, where learners have a great deal of scope to choose the skills and knowledge areas that are most important to them, found 42 categories of contract topics. The top ten contract areas accounted for 67% of the contracts. They were:
>
> Ability to use and to understand particular company procedures – 11%
> Computer skills – 11%
> Presentation skills (including meetings skills, and written presentations) – 10%
> Time management – 8%
> Training – 6%
> Assertiveness – 5%
> Budgeting – 5%
> Interviewing skills – 5%
> Performance appraisal – 3%
> Managing change – 3%
>
> Thompson 1994 (note, figures have been rounded)
>   No two learning contracts are exactly alike, and even two learning contracts in the same broad area are likely to exhibit significantly different features in their learning objectives, assessment measures and action plan.

- reflecting on the differences between the specific situation in which they practise the skill and other situations
- targeting increased understanding of the general application of the skill
- developing action plans for applying the skill in other situations.

Staged improvement

A key principle in using learning contracts for skill development is that the development of all skills takes place in stages. If I am new to working by persuasion and co-operation, for example, I am unlikely to become expert in the course of three or four weeks. I can, however, improve on my initial level of ability. The metaphor of a staircase illustrates this point (Figure 2.4). As a novice at persuasion I am at the foot of the stairs. A short learning contract may help me to climb three or four steps: it is unlikely to take me to the top of the flight. I am, however, likely to climb more quickly with the use of a learning contract than without one.

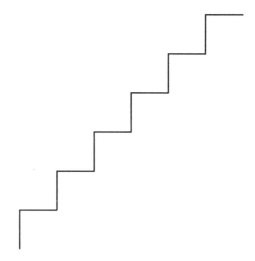

Figure 2.4   **Staged improvement**

Learning contracts for developing skills are often most successful when it is possible to establish attainable, clearly defined targets over relatively short periods of time. Small changes in behaviour may be the aim (i.e. to climb two, three or four steps up the scale from the present level of skill, towards greater competence).

The difficulties of skill development

If the foregoing sections seem to take an approach which is a little mechanical, perhaps a little *too* rational, it is because their purpose is to sketch out the basis of a practical route for the development of skills, not to provide a description of the entire journey.

Learners progress through the Learning Cycle in many different states of mind, sometimes in the state of cool and rational contemplation that is perhaps implied in the brief description above, but sometimes in alternating moods of confusion, elation, frustration, illumination and relief.

We can take giant strides towards the understanding and analysis of specific (and generic) skills, but in many areas our definitions will be imprecise. The metaphor of the staircase is a helpful model of progressive stages, but in reality the learning curve is not so regular, and at the outset, for the learner, the steps may seem to ascend into the darkness of the unknown.

It is a good idea for those of us who work with people, to help them develop their skills through learning contracts, to undertake some deliberate

Box 2.4 A critical model

An approach to general skills contracts is to break the skill down into some of its component parts.

Kate and Ken Back (1991) set out numerous useful models of effective behaviour for difficult situations. For example, it is not always easy to provide constructive criticism of the work of another person: the Backs' model for giving criticism breaks this skill down into seven stages:

1. Check that your inner dialogue is sound.
2. Check that your criticism is specific and not a personal attack.
3. Introduce the topic and, if appropriate, say why you want to raise it.
4. Make your specific criticism.
5. Get a response to your criticism.
6. Ask for suggestions to bring about the desired change.
7. Summarize the suggestions to be actioned.

This is followed by more detailed advice for each stage.

The use of an appropriate model of good practice of this sort in a learning contract can provide a firm foundation for making a balanced assessment of personal needs and then satisfying them.

skill development ourselves, in areas we find difficult, on a regular basis. It improves our ability to empathize with our clients, and prevents us from forgetting these other dimensions of the learning process. Juch (1983) provides a useful warning about some of these dimensions:

> Firstly, the catchphrase 'self development' is grossly and glibly overused . . . Books and articles create unrealistic expectations and suggest that it is possible for almost everybody to be able to manage their own career just by deciding to embark on self development. This is not the case. Good intentions are not enough. Whether self development is at all possible depends on whether the person has spare capacity and spare energy as well. And even then, continuously and flexibly pursuing a programme of self development against the odds of daily life is not easy. A strong motivation and great perseverance are required to overcome delays and setbacks in perceivable results.

Learning contracts help the individual to develop, but the energy, capacity, motivation and perseverance to which Juch refers are still required.

Contracts and competences

In recent years competence models have been developed which aim to define the abilities that people need in order to be effective at work. Models have been developed for specific occupations, as well as for general activities, including management and counselling, and models of the key skills needed for 'personal effectiveness' (Boyatzis 1982; IRS 1993; Matthewman 1996; Karpin 1995; Mansfield and Mitchell 1996).

There are two broad types of model, sometimes described as *attributes models* and *outcomes models*:

- competences as skills, or attributes, anchored to descriptions of behaviour
- competence standards, defining and describing what a person in a particular job role is expected to achieve, or the expected outcomes.

Sometimes attempts are made to signal differences between the contents of these models by calling the former competen*cies*, and the latter competen*ces*, but here we shall not trouble with so slight a distinction.

Both of these approaches to competence concern behaviour at work, and both go to some lengths to define the behaviour in such a way that it can be recognized. In that respect, they create models of good practice that can be used to guide development and assess performance.

Individual needs for development differ from learner to learner. A relevant competence model – whether specific to a company or generic to a job role or activity – can provide a framework for an analysis and a definition of individual needs.

The growth of competence-based training programmes in the UK in recent years seems to be one of the factors giving rise to an increased use of learning contracts. Competence-based programmes carry within them an implication that learning needs will differ from individual to individual, and that a similar diversity will characterize opportunities for development, being so firmly rooted in the circumstances of the individual workplace. Learning contracts can be extremely effective in this situation. Certain issues arise, however, when they are used with a competence model.

A large part of the power of the learning contract comes from the motivation it arouses in the learner, which comes from the learner's ownership and control of the contract. Where learners have the opportunity to define their own goals, and to exercise self-direction within broad limits, this high level of motivation can result in the achievement of great success. A competence model can affect the learner's sense of ownership – and hence their motivation.

To use a competence model successfully for learning and development, it is generally recognized that an adult learner must pass through a series of stages (Boyatzis 1982; Powers 1987), the first three of which are:

Box 2.5 Understanding the competences

On the MBA programme mentioned in Box 2.1, in the original design of 1989–1995, learners were required to undertake three overlapping learning contracts in areas defined by particular clusters of competences from the Boyatzis model (1982). They were advised to target development in between two and four competence behaviours, in contracts of duration between three and nine months.

The Boyatzis model was a generic model with a good research base, but the language in which it was expressed gave some learners great difficulty. Sometimes their confusion was obvious at an early stage, but on one occasion a learner whose contract included a commitment to improve his ability to 'develop and use symbols of group identity' had spent several weeks ostensibly working on the contract before betraying his lack of understanding of exactly what a 'symbol of group identity' was.

Another learner confused two different (but related) competence behaviours, and although he had agreed to work on the development of one of them, he was in fact trying to improve the other.

Both these events took place early in the life of the programme, before tutors had realized the extent of the scope for confusion. And in both cases the learners were making progress on development in other areas of their contracts!

When the MBA was revised in 1995, a different model of competence was incorporated within it.

---

1. Recognition of the relevant competence.
2. Understanding of the competence and how it relates to effective performance.
3. Carrying out a development needs analysis against the competence.

If some development is necessary, the individual then goes on to devise targets and an action plan for learning.

The first two stages are crucial, but are sometimes only partially achieved. Learners may have more difficulty understanding the competence model than tutors expect. The language may be obscure, the size and detail of the model may be barriers to comprehension (Beaumont 1995). Study of the model may seem to learners to be leading them away from a contemplation of their own performance in the workplace (and therefore away from areas where they want/need to develop). The model can act as a dark glass that has been set between the learner and their actual performance – obscuring their development needs rather than revealing them.

On programmes where regulations require a learner to address all the competences in a particular model, the motivational powers of learning

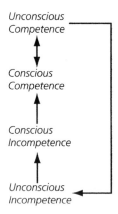

Figure 2.5   Stages in competence development

contracts are usually considerably diminished. Only when learners are allowed a degree of freedom to determine the direction of their own development are the full motivational benefits of learning contracts likely to be achieved.

If the intention of the programme is to use a complete competence model, tutors must be prepared to spend time, patience and ingenuity helping learners to recognize and understand it. Learners should be able to visualize and describe the competence in action, and to consider what different levels of attainment would look like. A model which incorporates established gradings of degrees of competence can be helpful (Spencer and Spencer 1993).

The importance of the stages of recognition, understanding and needs analysis can be reinforced by the use of a well-established model of competence development (Figure 2.5), which shows the first step in development being a move from a state of unconscious incompetence (unaware of good practice) to conscious incompetence (aware of good practice – as represented in the model – although not yet able to achieve it). The potential for slipping from unconscious competence (naturally effective performance) to unconscious incompetence highlights the importance of self-assessment at regular intervals.

Competence models can be used very successfully with learning contracts if the proper preparation is undertaken. In particular, when learners have already determined that they have a development need in a certain area, relevant selected parts of competence models can often serve as a basis for thinking about the exact nature of good practice.

Review

Developing skills and competences in the work environment, within the challenges of the job, is a particular strength of the learning contract method. The initial flexibility of the approach enables adaptation to the features of specific situations, while the detail of the written contract enables a clear, precise definition of what is to be achieved and how that will be assessed, sufficient to measure against a general standard of skill or competence.

These benefits are not experienced automatically, however, as soon as learning contracts are brought into use. At the heart of the learning contract method is an interaction between two (or more) individuals. The success of the method is not simply a matter of mechanics, but of skill. It is not enough just to use learning contracts: they must be used thoughtfully, carefully and skilfully.

Chapter 3

Design and development

Using learning contracts in any programme of learning or development involves decisions about design.

Learning contracts can be highly effective and motivational because of the range of choices they allow the individual learner, but the most effective contracts will have clear parameters within which learners can make choices. Establishing those parameters is a matter of design.

Decisions must also be made about the design of the whole programme. Is this a new programme, where the aims, structure, learning methods and timing can be set out afresh, starting on a blank sheet of paper? Or is it an established programme, where the learning contracts will replace some of the current methods of learning and assessment? In either of these cases, certain options for design should be recognized and evaluated. Whether you are considering launching a new programme, or contemplating modifications to an existing programme, there are likely to be some areas of flexibility and some areas of immovable constraint.

Most programme design and delivery is a social process: the co-operation of a number of people is usually required. There may be a need to encourage and to develop among members of the tutor team a common understanding of the contract method and how it will operate within the programme – perhaps by involving them in design decisions. Also, for the programme to be successful, it may be necessary to develop understanding on the part of the customers or clients, and perhaps involve them, or their representatives, at the design stage.

For the sake of exposition in this chapter we shall explore the design of the contract and the design of the programme one at a time, but in practice they interact with one another, so that decisions in one area will impact on the other, and neither can really be considered independently.

Designing the contract

In Chapter 1 we said that the key characteristics of learning contracts are focus and flexibility. Where they have been used most successfully, learning contracts have the following features:

1. They focus on learning: their objectives explicitly target the development of the learner's knowledge and/or skills.
2. They allow scope for individual choice on the part of the learner, and negotiation with a tutor (and/or the learner's line manager) about the objectives of the contract, how they are to be achieved, and the measures of performance that will be used to assess them. In terms of enhanced relevance, motivation and learning, the wider the range of choice for the individual, the better.
3. They are written agreements. The terms of the contract are set out in writing and agreed by all relevant parties. Setting the terms in writing generally leads to them being more precise.
4. They are assessed at an agreed point. There are performance measures and a deadline for completion, and the learner reports back on progress. The details of assessment will depend on the programme – but without assessment in some form, a key part of the learning contract is missing.

The freedom of the individual learner to design the contract is a powerful component of contract learning. Having taken a large hand in creating the contract, the learner feels ownership for it and is motivated to achieve its objectives. In most circumstances, however, it is likely to be desirable to provide some structural parameters to support this freedom of choice. Some of these aspects of design are mundane but necessary.

Scope: the specification of areas that can be covered in a learning contract is a key aspect of their design. Where very broad choices are afforded, the contracts are more likely to be owned by the learners. In other circumstances, participants on a programme may be required to tackle a learning contract in broad subject areas, e.g. Finance, Supervision, Information Technology (IT). This allows some choice and also ensures some systematic coverage of syllabus areas. This restriction of choice, by placing contracts in subject areas (Finance, IT, etc.) or by linking contracts to competence models, means that more work must usually be done with the learners in advance of them agreeing the contract, to give them a grounding in the subject area and to help them to understand the rules.

Timing: it can be useful to establish a notional length of time for the span of the contract (e.g. six weeks, three months or six months). It may also be helpful, particularly if the contract is part of a programme leading to a qualification, to estimate the amount of input time it will take the learner to complete the contract (e.g. 40 hours, 120 hours) or at least a minimum

Box 3.1 Parameters

The rules for learning contracts on a Certificate in Management Studies programme.

1. The learning contract must be about some aspect of management. This was designed to rule out the proposals by engineers to learn more about some aspect of engineering, and librarians to learn more about libraries.
2. It must be a learning contract. Its focus is individual learning, not the achievement of short-term work objectives, or changing the organization.
3. It must be a live proposal. It is not a summary, after the event, of learning objectives already achieved. The targets the learner hopes to achieve must be agreed in advance.
4. The initiative in establishing the goal and the objectives of the learning contract rests with the learner.
5. The learning contract is agreed by the learner, a tutor and a representative of the learner's employer – usually the line manager – and assessed by them.
6. At least one of the learning contracts (out of three) must be about some aspect of developing interpersonal skills.
7. The learning contract is expected to take about 40 hours to complete over a six- to eight-week period.

amount of time it is expected to take. These tend to be guidelines rather than rigid rules. It may also be desirable to establish a particular set time by which the learning contract must be agreed, and a date by which it should be assessed. These deadlines, which help to concentrate the learner's mind, will be made more specific in the agreements with each individual. It may be a requirement, for example, that a contract in a particular module is agreed by 15 January at the latest, and assessed no later than 20 March: one learner may arrange a meeting at which the contract is agreed on 10 January and set a completion date of 1 March.

Format: there should be a given format for the written learning contract, containing, for example, headings of Goal, Learning Objectives, Action Plan, Resources, Assessment and Completion Date. A simple format can be set out on one page – as in Figure 3.1. If the proposal is likely to be more substantial – if it is, for example, to be the basis of a longer and more complex contract – a form can still be helpful, but if learners' proposals are likely to be modified or amended during negotiations with the tutor, it is much easier to encourage the use of a word-processing package wherever possible, for

Name:... Telephone:.................. Ref No:..........
Start Date:........................... Completion Date:.................. ....

AIM:

Learning Objectives	Action Plan	Assessment

Resources

Signed:

Participant   Line Manager   Tutor

Figure 3.1   Example of a simple learning contract form

Box 3.2 Further restrictions

Sometimes further restrictions can make a contract more effective.

Managers undertaking the Northern Regional Management Centre's Certificate in Management Studies were required to devise one learning contract (out of three) on some aspect of interpersonal (IP) skills. British Gas North Eastern, who worked in partnership with NRMC for several years to provide the programme for BGNE managers, required the learners to make the interpersonal skills learning contract the first one of the three.

In the opinion of the tutors, both these restrictions had beneficial effects on the programme.

Interpersonal skills are essential to effective management, yet those least able in this area are often those least likely to propose an interpersonal skills contract.

The restriction is not particularly confining – there are still many choices to be made.

Managers in the BGNE scheme who tackled the IP skills contract first were more likely than managers in other organizations to continue to explore and develop interpersonal skills in their second and third contracts.

ease of amendment, following a set of specified headings. If learners have easy access to a computer, this makes sense even for shorter proposals.

Responsibilities: the responsibilities of the different parties should be made clear. For example, clarity is needed about who is responsible for proposing the first draft of the learning contract (it is best if it is the learner), and what resources they may expect from the tutor and/or from their employer in support of their work. These specific points may be framed within a complete philosophy of responsibility for learning, if the contracts are used in an explicit context of self-directed learning. Any specific rules in this area should be clear and simple, and ideally, few in number.

Free choice for the learner is supported by firm decisions taken in each of these areas. It is usually beneficial to set out these points as rules of the contracting process, to which all parties can refer as a basic structure for the agreement.

Delivering the learning contract

Design decisions must be taken about each of the key activities involved in delivering the contract (Figure 3.2).

- *Preparation* involves two activities – priming, or briefing the learners,

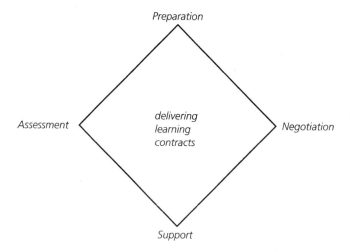

Figure 3.2   Activities involved in delivering the contract

and helping them to make decisions about the focus of their contracts. Priming of some sort is essential – all the more so if this is the first time learners have used learning contracts. Decisions need to be taken about how and when the learners will be primed, and who will do the priming. Helping them to make decisions about the focus of their contract may entail some supported needs analysis. The tutor, or the team of tutors, needs to decide whether some structured form of needs analysis will be provided for learners. These activities are discussed in more detail in Chapters 4 and 5.

- *Negotiation* involves agreeing the contract with the learner. Decisions are needed about who will negotiate the contract, and how that process will be managed. It may be reasonable to expect that agreement can be reached in a single meeting, or it may take several meetings and several drafts of the contract before all the necessary work has been done. Depending on the level at which contracts are being used, and the range of choices available to the learner, tutors may need to involve other subject specialists: how will this be achieved? In work-based contracts, should an employer's representative take part in the negotiation? What role should they play? How will they be briefed for this role? Successful negotiation is at the heart of effective learning contracts, and it is discussed in more detail in Chapters 6, 7, 8 and 9. The involvement of employers' representatives is discussed in Chapter 12.

- *Support*: once the contract is under way, will it be supported? If so, to what degree, and with what resources? This may be partly a question of the resources available to tutors and learners, and of course it can have a practical impact on the possible scope of learning contracts. A learner who wishes to learn how to use a computer, for example, must have access to the relevant equipment: does the tutor, or the programme team, intend to provide this access? Will specialist inputs be provided for learners – special workshops or classes on the area they wish to study? In most cases the potential diversity of learning contract study areas means that supporting inputs will be limited to what is easily available: therefore it is useful for tutors to explore in advance exactly what resources and support *are* available. There are also decisions to be taken about whether there will be support-group meetings or tutorials during the course of the contract, to review progress and boost morale. There is more discussion of support in Chapter 10.

- *Assessment*: finally, decisions must be taken about how the contracts will be assessed. The details of assessment will be subject to agreement between individual tutors and learners, but the range of possible means of assessment is often a design and policy decision, particularly if the contract is part of a programme that leads to a qualification. In such cases, examination regulations often form a significant limiting factor. For example, tutor and learner may want to incorporate an oral presentation or interview into the assessment – but the regulations of the institution may require that all assessment is by written report. In programmes leading to qualifications, it is important at the design stage to share ideas on assessment with all the tutors who will be involved in negotiating and assessing learning contracts – ideally with all the tutors who are working on the programme – and reach agreement on suitable and acceptable means. Assessment is discussed in more detail in Chapters 8 and 11.

Programme design

Certain key decisions need to be taken about the design of the programme which provides the context of the learning contracts. Whether it is an established programme or one which is to be newly designed, it must have a purpose, a market, an outline content and a schedule.

Perhaps the simplest design for a programme using learning contracts is one which provides an initial period of priming and needs analysis, followed by the agreement of the learning contract, followed by action in carrying out the contract, and then assessment.

A short personal development programme can be designed along these broad lines, for example, as in Figure 3.3 (page 36), with a contract period of six weeks, during which time the learners take action to develop the skills they have targeted in the contract. This is still a broad outline, of course, lacking detail on how the learners are primed and how their needs are to be analysed.

Figure 3.3   A simple design

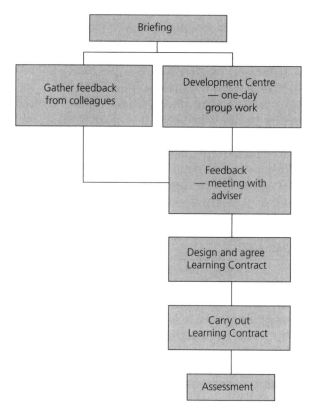

Figure 3.4   A management development programme

Figure 3.4 provides more detail. Designed specifically for senior managers in small and medium-sized businesses, this programme used an intensive one-day development centre and evaluative questionnaires from work col-

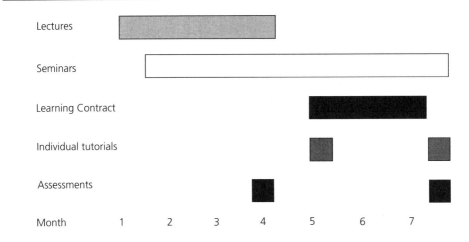

Figure 3.5   **A learning contract as part of a longer programme of study**

leagues to assess skill development needs. The initial briefing was delivered through a short presentation to which prospective participants were invited. The learning contract was scheduled to last for six weeks, and was supported by an interim meeting with a tutor after three weeks.

In this example much time was spent on a deliberate and structured analysis of development needs. This is not necessary in every case of using learning contracts. In other circumstances, such as in academic, educational courses, rather than 'needs analysis' it will be more appropriate to talk about the learners 'establishing their priorities', or 'developing their research proposal' or simply 'deciding on the contract area'.

An educational programme of study – say a module within a degree programme – might follow a structure as in Figure 3.5 (above). In this case, the first part of the module is delivered through lectures and seminars covering core materials, and there is an assessment at the end of the lecture programme. The second part of the course is taken up with a long learning contract, agreed at an individual tutorial, supported by a continuing programme of seminar meetings, and assessed partly in writing and partly at a final individual tutorial.

The easiest way of fitting learning contracts into existing qualification programmes is to use them to support or to replace projects.

Learning contracts will only work properly if the ground has been prepared, so that learners are forewarned and can think about what they want to do. Thought needs to be given to the timing of the first briefing sessions, and how learners can be stimulated to choose a subject area that they will value. In the example in Figure 3.5, learners are told of the contract at the outset of the module, and receive some guidance then on the range of choices available to them. As the beginning of the contract period

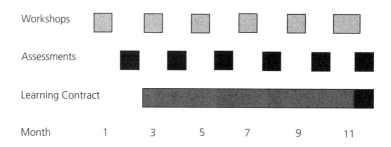

Figure 3.6   **A postgraduate diploma**

approaches, more time is spent in lectures and seminars, priming the learners to develop a contract proposal.

There are benefits in assigning learning contracts a clear start date within the programme (to apply to the whole group) and a clear end date. With longer learning contracts, some slippage in the start date may be permissible, which allows for re-drafting of proposals.

Another model, used on a postgraduate diploma programme for part-time students, combines a long contract period (of up to nine months) with a series of workshops and short assessments (Figure 3.6). The contract is about some aspect of personal development, based on a competency model. The learners spend the first two months of the programme working with the competency model and gathering feedback on their strengths and weaknesses, before they set out the contract.

In our examples so far there has been only one learning contract. There is evident value, however, in using several learning contracts on a programme – not least because of the scope this gives for helping the individual to develop skills as a learner. It is noticeable that with the second and subsequent contracts learners are usually better equipped to take the initiative in designing the proposal and exercising greater ownership over the contract (Thompson 1994).

As a final example of a programme structure, the one-year certificate programme represented in Figure 3.7 combines coverage of four core areas – through a mixture of group workshops and distance learning materials – with three short learning contracts, each of six to eight weeks in length. Learners complete written assessments in each core area, as well as being

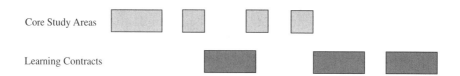

Figure 3.7   **Multiple learning contracts**

assessed on their learning contracts. In the original design of the programme, the learners completed all four core areas before beginning the contracts, but bringing the first contract forward was found to increase motivation and interest.

To summarize the design decisions illustrated by these examples, we must decide: how many contracts will there be? What is their scope? How long will they be? What other forms of learning will there be? What other forms of assessment will there be? What is the overall shape of the programme?

Purpose and values

It is often valuable to have a clear view of the main aims of using learning contracts in the context of the aims of the programme. This can be a helpful touchstone when it comes to solving detailed design and implementation problems. If the programme is designed and delivered by a team of people, then it is very valuable to reach a consensus, if possible, on these matters. This section raises some of these issues and some of the potential conflicts.

1. By their nature, learning contracts can permit individual choice about areas for study and development: this exercise of individual choice appears to be a feature of productive adult learning (Knowles 1986). One purpose of using learning contracts in a programme might therefore be to help individuals develop their own learning skills. Tutors attaching a high priority to this aspect of the learning contract are likely to put more emphasis on the individual learners taking responsibility for the different stages of the contract process, and would perhaps also encourage reflection on the part of the learners about their use of their learning skills.

   There may be conflicts between some of the values inherent in learning contracts, or between these values and the purpose and values of the overall programme.

2. Another feature of learning contracts is that they allow the design of quite individual programmes of study – and therefore each individual on a development programme can address their unique, specific learning needs. A tutor, or a programme team, placing emphasis on this aspect of the learning contract may be more likely to suggest, advise (or even, in some cases, prescribe) particular learning contracts for particular learners. But this runs counter to placing a high value on self-directed learning: which is more important to the programme team?

3. Lawrence (1994) writes of the difficulty of integrating a taught course with experiential learning. There may be conflicts in values between the learning contract component of a programme – where the learner is expected to take active responsibility – and other parts of the programme – where they may be expected to take a more passive role. Lawrence is

writing in the context of action learning, which is more difficult to integrate with a taught course than contract learning, but these conflicts still remain to be considered, and the transitions need to be managed.

4. Learning contracts provide a way of helping people to develop relevant skills. If the tutors who are using contracts place a high value on this, they may need to consider how far this is in harmony with the overall programme. Other tutors – and perhaps the learners themselves – may see the main purpose and value of the programme as being the acquisition of knowledge and understanding, and they may resent and resist the introduction of contracts to develop skills.

5. Work-based learning contracts enable the learner's employer to be involved in agreeing the contract. The programme team might consider this to be of great importance. If so then, logically, time and effort should be put into briefing the employer. However, the employer might look for short-term returns from the learning contract – using it to get the learner to tackle immediate work projects which offer little learning. This can run counter to the principles of self-directed learning, and to learning being the main object of the contract: how can these conflicts be resolved?

6. Whenever learning contracts are incorporated into qualification programmes, a number of purpose and value issues are likely to arise. Course regulations are likely to impose a number of requirements and contraints on the contract – such as the need to study certain ideas, books and papers as part of undertaking the contract; the need to provide evidence of completion of the contract in certain specified formats; and the nature of assessment (for example, a grading structure may be required). The higher the qualification, the greater the number of terms that will be imposed on the contract.

   These impositions can run counter to the desires and wishes of the learner in undertaking the contract, and to the aims of the individual tutor in using contract learning. For some learners the main aim may become to gain the qualification, even at the expense (if necessary) of valuable learning and development. It is wise for tutors to develop intelligent views on the purpose and values of learning contracts in this context, and to reach an accommodation with the necessary constraints. We shall explore this subject further in Chapters 8 and 11, on assessment.

7. Different priorities often attach to different positions in relation to a programme. Since the late 1980s in the UK there has been an increasing number of joint ventures between educational institutions and employing organizations to deliver programmes that incorporate learning in the workplace and recognized academic qualifications. These ventures bring together onto a programme team representatives of the partners in the venture, and in a variation of the problems of communi-

---

Box 3.3 Purpose and values

Assessment is an area where it is useful to have a clear view of purposes and values. As assessment is both the point at the end of a contract where its results can be evaluated, and also central to the award of qualifications, it can be a point at which differences in opinion are starkly expressed.

Within a programme team, opinions may differ about the value of assessment. The argument presented in this book, for example, that assessment is an essential part of an effective learning contract, is not recognized by everyone as a universal truth, and traditional academics may look askance on the methods of assessing contracts which are suggested later in Chapters 8 and 11.

When learning contracts are introduced into an established course, they are often introduced into one module, at the instigation of the tutor in charge of that study area.

Some members of a programme team will be suspicious of attempts to include assessment of a learning contract in the overall assessment of the programme – they may be unable to see beyond traditional methods of assessment, which typically compares like with like (i.e. everyone does the same assignment).

If the learning contract has been introduced in order to do something radical, such as to develop personal or interpersonal skills in the context of an academic course (as opposed to the analytical skills which can be demonstrated in assignments and examinations), the traditionalists will be even more doubtful.

And with contracts in these areas, some other staff members may feel that attempts to assess the contracts can subvert the process of self-development, which is at the heart of the learning contract: they, too, are bound by a relatively traditional perspective – albeit a different one.

---

cation and conflict between members of the learning triangle described at the beginning of Chapter 2, there may be clashes of priorities. The employers' representatives may see the university/college team as, on the whole, too remote from workplace concerns, too academic and bureaucratic, whereas the employers' group may be seen as too concerned with the short term, blind to longer-term issues of transferable skills, and too concerned with inputs and experience, while naïve about how skills and abilities can be measured.

Where these differences are resolved, and an effective working relationship develops, the team may encounter further difficulties as the programme is implemented, with more academic-minded members of the institution and more task-oriented managers from the organization.

In conclusion, there are no easy solutions to the problems raised in this section. The extent to which they will impact on any particular programme will depend on a number of factors, including the expertise, interest and motivation of the people who are involved. With a small team of like-minded people, a clear statement of purpose and values can be developed and agreed, and used as a point of reference. With a larger, more disparate team the champions of learning contracts may have a longer journey to make before they succeed in influencing their colleagues. Where learning contracts are introduced into existing programmes it is wise to consider how they can be aligned with the stated purpose of the programme, with the desires of the clients, and with statements of value and intent from within the institution.

Review

Effective learning contracts combine flexibility with focus, allowing considerable choice to the learner about the target area of learning and development. The exercise of this choice is enhanced by providing a firm structure to the learning contract. The business of designing the parameters of learning contracts is inextricably bound to the design of the programme in which they are based, and issues of how and where they will fit into the total programme.

In taking design decisions, it is important to develop a clear view of the purpose of the programme and the priorities in using learning contracts within it. Clear, shared values can point the way to solutions to the problems that can arise during design and implementation.

In designing the contract and the programme that surrounds it, it must be remembered that using learning contracts involves four key activities:

- preparation
- negotiation
- support
- assessment.

There are more details of these activities in the chapters that follow.

Chapter 4

Priming

The initiative in proposing the content of a particular learning contract should lie with the person who will do the learning. Without some preliminary guidance and help from the tutor, however, it is likely that the learning contract will take up more time and produce fewer real results than otherwise. The help that the learner needs can be divided into two types:

- priming – which means a clear briefing as to the role he/she is expected to play, and some encouragement to do so
- needs analysis – which means some help in selecting a suitable area of knowledge or skill for development.

Needs analysis is the subject of the following chapter. This chapter considers priming.

At its very least, priming simply means providing a clear brief to the learner about what he/she is expected to do. The most effective priming inspires the learner to explore areas in which he/she could learn and develop and leads to a clear and thoughtful written proposal for a contract. With effective priming, learners will indeed take ownership of the learning contract from the outset, and produce proposals that they are keen to follow through. When priming fails, the time and cost necessary to agree a learning contract proposal can double, while the noticeable benefit may actually decrease.

Priming can be broken down into three activities:

- explaining what a learning contract is and why it is being used
- building confidence in the use of the learning contract
- making clear what the learner has to do.

Best-practice priming will deliberately focus attention on each of these areas.

What and why

We have already seen that a learning contract is a simple agreement between a learner and a tutor which specifies what will be learned, how and when that learning will be measured, what activities will be undertaken to achieve the learning and what resources will be used.

We have discussed some of the general reasons for using learning contracts and the benefits that can accrue from their use. In any particular scheme or programme there will be specific advantages which can be raised with the learners.

This, the *what* and *why*, should be a central part of the briefing to learners approaching learning contracts for the first time.

Using a blank copy of a standard contract form is a very good way of introducing a learning contract. A blank form is usually a better introduction than an example of a completed contract proposal. Devoid of illustrative – and probably irrelevant – content, the blank form poses questions and offers initiatives. Examples may be useful at a later stage of the introduction, when learners have a grasp of the aims of the contract process, and the format of the contract proposal.

An obvious benefit of learning contracts is that they enable each individual learner to undertake the programme of study or development of their choice. By giving examples of the range of contract areas that can be undertaken (or that have been undertaken by learners in the past), the tutor can illustrate the scale of choice that is available.

It is also often beneficial to explain the educational reasons for using learning contracts. Knowles's ideas on the characteristics of effective adult learners as described in Chapter 1 can provide a useful talking point.

In work-based learning, the use of learning contracts is founded on sound theories of how people learn and develop skills, and on a set of beliefs about the value of learning from real experiences in the workplace. In particular, an introduction to the Learning Cycle and its relationship to contract learning can result in clearly defined benefits.

- Learners are more likely to accept the contract approach. The theory base is easy to understand, generally conforms with their experience, and has rational connections with the learning contract method.
- Learners are more likely to undertake skills-based contracts requiring real action in the workplace.
- Learners are better able to structure the learning contract proposal in Planning, Action, Reflection and Knowledge terms.
- This approach also helps to answer some questions about assessment that are usually posed at this point.

When using learning contracts to help people to develop skills in the workplace, it can be particularly helpful to emphasize the introspective, developmental aspect of the learning contract approach. Most learners will be familiar with work projects and performance targets and the danger from the outset is that the learning contract – which is about learning and personal development – will be confused with a project – which is about doing, or about acquiring and analysing facts. The skill-development aspects of the learning contract approach should be emphasized to correct this misapprehension at an early stage.

In addition to explaining the *what* and the *why* in general terms it is, of course, desirable to brief learners on the role of learning contracts in the particular programme or scheme in which they are placed. Positive reasons for the use of learning contracts must be communicated at this point, or the learners will be disinclined to invest the necessary preparatory effort.

It is advisable for the tutor to brief the learner personally, face-to-face, whether individually or in a group of fellow learners. This is almost always necessary, to generate the required impact to move learners to devise their own contract proposals. Printed material – in the form of information and instructions – is useful support but is rarely sufficient by itself.

Confidence and motivation

The second function of priming is to encourage the learner to feel confident in the learning contract approach and to be motivated to use it.

Some aspects of motivation will be affected by details of the particular scheme: for example, are people being invited to use learning contracts or compelled to do so? What are the consequences of success or failure?

Motivation generally is enhanced by:

- clearly placing responsibility for taking the initiative with the learner
- specifying clear targets to be met (a proposal, in a particular form, by a certain date)
- helping the learner to clarify what can be learned, and what should be learned (through the process of needs analysis, discussed in Chapter 5).

Nevertheless, learners will often approach their first learning contract with a degree of trepidation and doubt. This may not be apparent to the person providing the briefing, but it is safe to assume that a little time can be well spent on building confidence in the following areas.

- *The method*

Some examples of the successes achieved by using learning contracts are worth as much as the explanation of the educational foundation of the method. Stewart-David's quotation from an undergraduate student is perhaps not untypical of learners' potential first impressions:

My initial reaction was one of reticence and hostility. I thought to myself

---

Box 4.1 Motivating learners

The context of the priming presentation will have an effect on the learners' motivation before the tutor first opens his or her mouth.

Consider, for example, the situation where the learners have already signed up to undertake the module which contains the learning contract, as part of a course that will lead to a valued qualification. Imagine that in order to complete the module, there is no alternative to undertaking the contract. These circumstances will provide a certain level of (extrinsic) motivation.

Compare this with the situation where a group of potential learners listen to a tutor explain a programme that they may, or may not, choose to undertake. The expected benefit is purely that of self-development – there is no qualification attached to the programme. All things being equal, this tutor will need to work harder to convince the audience of the value of the contract approach.

---

that this was going to be an attempt to employ 'modern' but previously untested approaches to learning and developing oneself. It was us who were going to be the guinea pigs. (Stewart-David 1993)

- *The potential*

Some suggestion of goals that can be achieved can reinforce positive attitudes towards development. Illustrating the range of subject matter which can be tackled by the contract can indicate the scope for pursuing personal goals. When using skill development contracts, the tutor should be aware that learners can find it easy to think of firm, unchanging lines that separate things they can do from things they are 'no good at'. It is often worth spending a little time challenging this belief.

- *The people*

Confidence comes from knowing one is in safe hands. Experienced tutors will communicate the fact that they have used these methods before. It may be desirable to organize direct endorsements from happy and successful learners from previous programmes. New tutors should rely on the past success of the method elsewhere, make sure they get all the details of their explanations correct, and exude an air of quiet competence.

At this stage of priming it is important to remember that people are not entirely rational, logical, trusting beings. As well as hearing explanations, they need to be persuaded, motivated and (here and there) reassured: other people have done this, and it works; you can do it, if you want to; no one's perfect, we can all improve: in the end, it's up to you.

Box 4.2 Staged improvement

It is natural, but dangerous, to take a static position on our current level of skill. This can dictate our response to such areas as new technology ('I'm no good at computing'), finance ('I'm no good at numbers') and interpersonal skills ('I'm no good at negotiating').

The 'I'm no good at . . .' position is essentially a static one.

The more thoughtful aspect of this argument is based on the observation that some people are 'naturally' better at computing/finance/negotiating etc. than others. Is it, then, possible for those others to be effective leaders/expert negotiators/good team members?

When faced with this reaction, my response is that:

- Most people can learn quite difficult skills to some degree. (Driving a car, using a costing system, communicating in a foreign language, for example, are all complex acquired skills.)
- Nearly all people can improve their skills to some extent in areas of deficiency or need. (I may not become an expert computer technologist, an accountant or a professional negotiator, but I can develop my skills in each of these areas.)

In skill development contracts, it is often helpful to use the metaphor of the flight of stairs as a visual aid (as in Chapter 2) to illustrate the concept of staged improvement.

At the foot of the stairs on the ground floor is total ignorance of the skill area. At the head of the stairs is complete mastery. A single learning contract may progress me upwards several steps. So by undertaking a learning contract I am not proposing to achieve expertise by the end of it, but I expect to improve on my present level of skills – whatever that level is. This simple illustration has had a marvellous effect on learners' confidence and motivation.

- *Disclosure*

The learner's confidence is also boosted in most cases by those around him or her taking a positive, honest approach to strengths and weaknesses. In an atmosphere where an admission of ignorance or lack of skill is seen as a confession of sin there will be few honest self-evaluations, but if a learner can see that it is quite acceptable to set out to improve certain areas of knowledge or skills there is more chance of an honest and accurate basis for the contract.

In programmes which include work-based learning, the tutor who is providing the briefing must take into account the working environment of the learner when encouraging disclosure. People other than the tutor deter-

---

Box 4.3 Unforgivable sins

In most companies there are degrees of inadmissibility of weakness.

Even in highly task-orientated companies it is okay to confess to the need for more knowledge about how other parts of the company work. This is called 'business awareness', and the lack of it can be blamed on other people for not sharing the information, and on the fact that my section has been asked to produce 150% for the last six months.

Next, in many companies, is information technology. Depending on the level of penetration it may be acceptable to want to start from scratch, or it may be a case of wanting to learn how to handle particular types of information on the computer.

About the same level of venial sin is the new technical area I have just taken over – I've just moved into marketing/personnel/technical services and I need to acquire a working knowledge of the techniques quickly.

To the junior managers who have just acquired responsibility for recruitment or appraisal and/or for giving major presentations, and so on, the novelty of the responsibility can sanction the desire to take on a contract in this area.

It is the person who has been in charge of a team for years who finds it most difficult to admit the need to develop team skills.

In an unsympathetic task-orientated company, the atmosphere conspires with the personal difficulty – often to prevent learners improving the skills they need most.

---

mine the degree of disclosure which is 'safe' – particularly the learner's boss and his/her colleagues in the workplace, as well as fellow learners. The tutor can have some influence, but may need to proceed with caution.

The learner's role

So far we have briefed the learner on the learning contract method and we have paid some attention to matters of motivation and confidence. It is also necessary to provide a clear picture of what we want the learner to do. In particular, we can predict and pre-empt the following questions from learners.

- *The subject of the learning contract.* How much choice do they have? Is it a completely free choice? Are they expected to consult with someone – such as a colleague on the programme? A learning set? Their own

---

Box 4.4 The unquantifiable

Phil was a design engineer by background and had recently become a team leader in an engineering concern. He was well motivated to tackle the development programme, but he appeared shy, precise, more than a little self-conscious, and uneasy in undertaking the required learning contract to develop aspects of his interpersonal skills.

At the negotiation and conclusion of the learning contract he used the word 'Quantifiable' as though it were entirely synonymous with 'Assessable'.

As well as Phil and the tutor, Phil's line manager was involved in agreeing the contract. Of a similar background, he also expressed discomfort at making explicit judgements about non-quantitative areas, and they moved swiftly back to the safety of the world of numbers for the next learning contract. The main concern of both Phil and his line manager seemed to be to frame the contract in terms amenable to clear, numerical assessment, rather than considering Phil's priority areas for learning.

(Even among design engineers, this is an extreme case.)

---

manager? Are there any methods of needs analysis they are expected to use? Are they bound by the results of these methods?

- *The timing.* When do they produce the proposal? How much preparation time do they have? How much time will they have to complete the learning contract, i.e. how 'big' is it? Is there a deadline date for completion?
- *The format.* What should their proposal look like? What headings, or prepared forms, should they use?
- *The people.* Who will agree the proposal? Who will assess the completed contract?
- *Assessment.* How will the contract be assessed? What will they need to produce in order to succeed at the contract? For skills development contracts: how are they expected to demonstrate their development?
- *The outcome.* What happens if the contract is judged not satisfactory? If this is part of a qualification: what contribution will this make to their overall grades?

These are all questions the tutor must be able to answer clearly to reassure learners that there is a firm structure supporting the relatively free choices they are asked to make.

In skills development contracts, there will be questions about how certain skills might be assessed – particularly interpersonal skills. An early focus on assessment, however, can lead to learning contracts being driven into areas where measures of performance are easier. These will rarely corre-

---

Box 4.5 Examples of priming systems

Approaches to priming will naturally depend upon the particular scheme of which the learning contract is a part.

One management development scheme provides for a priming presentation two months before the deadline date for agreeing the learning contract. The intervening two months is partly taken up with common, foundation studies, but there are also activities the learner is recommended to undertake to devise a proposal. The learning contract is scheduled to run for six to eight weeks.

In a second scheme, based on a short (twelve-week) part-time course, the group was primed at the first meeting and then a 'trial learning contract' was undertaken by each person in the group. The proposal was drafted there and then by each person, and discussed with a colleague, but was not individually agreed with the tutor. This trial learning contract was small – three weeks appears to be an optimum time. The group reviewed results in a second workshop that also included new material. After two or three workshops, and two or three 'trial learning contracts' whose subject might be chosen out of curiosity or whim, an individually negotiated contract was established for each person, to run over a two-month period.

In this case the trial contracts and the reflection and feedback on them provided excellent priming for the learners, many of whom were then able to produce clear and effective proposals for the final learning contract.

---

spond to actual development needs. The tutor should advise the learners to consider their development needs first, and give assurances that methods of assessment can always be agreed, whatever the area in question.

Methods of priming

The priming process can be long or short, depending on the programme, the time and resources available, and the abilities of the learners. A presentation to a group of learners is a cost-effective method of face-to-face explanation. A presentation covering all the points in this chapter, with time allowed for questions, can be carried out in 45 minutes.

If the learners are very new to flexible approaches to learning, or if the parameters of the contract are complex, the tutor will need to return to matters explained in the priming presentation and re-state or elaborate on them. Part of the process of negotiating a contract can be reminding learners of the benefits of the contract process, the parameters and the rules. A priming presentation to learners, therefore, should be regarded as a first, substantial step in teaching them about the contract process, but one which is unlikely to make experts of them.

It is advisable to prepare printed briefing material as well as an oral explanation: a brief learning contract guide can include a summary of the process, the rules and parameters, examples of contract areas, and the contract form.

Review

Priming is a necessary part of the structure that supports the learning contract, but its importance can too easily be overlooked. The learning contract method is different in significant ways to other, more common, approaches to training or self-development, and it is necessary to introduce it in a manner that communicates its differences and its potential.

The period of priming gives learners the chance to prepare themselves for the responsibility of taking an active part in designing their own programme of learning. At the same time, they may be given help to decide what their contracts should target: this is the subject of the following chapter.

Chapter 5

Learning needs analysis

Most learning contract schemes provide learners with some choice about what they would like to study or develop for their contracts, and so before approaching a tutor to define the terms of the contract, learners need to make some decisions about their priorities, their wants and their needs.

Having primed learners about the use of the learning contract, as discussed in the previous chapter, tutors may consider the provision of structured methods to help the learner select suitable areas of knowledge or skill for development.

This process is perhaps easier in programmes which are essentially designed to enhance knowledge and understanding. Where the contract is a way of structuring a research project, for example, this stage consists of the students identifying options and deciding on their relative levels of interest in them. The tutor may stimulate this process by providing ideas about possible areas of study. Students may consider the implications of their choice for the remainder of the programme – for example, the possibility of using a learning contract to explore a particular area which might later provide a sound basis for a dissertation – and the tutor may be able to advise in this respect.

Where programmes and contracts are designed primarily to improve skills and enhance performance, the choice of a contract area should logically include some audit of current levels of skills, or current quality of performance, in order to identify priority learning needs. This is often a complex matter. Most of this chapter concerns needs analysis in this latter context of programmes and learning contracts that aim to develop skills, although there are sections in the early pages which are equally applicable to both types of programme.

Priorities for learning

The learner's decision concerning priorities for the learning contract may be completely unassisted by the tutor. The learner can simply be primed to prepare a proposal for a learning contract, and the derivation of the area for development left to his/her discretion.

In some cases this can be very effective: the learner identifies areas of interest, or problem areas for development, and brings them to the negotiation. This is the epitome of self-directed (i.e. unassisted) learning. In most cases, however, the process benefits from some guidance and support. The simplest form of this guidance is to offer a menu of options. Most education and training providers are familiar with menu systems. Academic institutions provide options, electives and choices between alternative assignments. Most training departments operate a menu system to publicize the programmes that employees may undertake. When it comes to learning contracts, provision of a list of study or skill areas from which a learner might choose may seem a good idea: it will open the learner's eyes to the wide range of topics that can be studied, or skills that can be developed.

The simple menu system is not really a method of needs analysis at all, of course, and it may lead to choices being made on the basis of curiosity, novelty or interest. Depending on the aims of the programme, this may be entirely acceptable, as long as the learner's interest is confirmed and consolidated during the process of negotiating the contract, so that a topic chosen out of curiosity isn't quickly abandoned unfinished.

The menu of topics set out for learners may simply be an extension of what tutors have been achieving through the parts of the programme that have preceded the learning contract: informing and (perhaps) intriguing learners with ideas and facts in their area of interest. As the programme moves from a phase of tutor-direction to the learning contract, which will be learner-directed, the tutor sets out a range of directions which the contracts may take. Here the tutor should make a clear distinction between what is mandatory – i.e. the rules or limitations of the contract – and what is merely provided as an example. Learners can sometimes be confused if they are provided with a range of examples at too early a stage in their acquaintance with learning contracts. For this reason it is sometimes helpful if any early menu of examples indicates only broad contract areas, and does not provide examples of detailed learning objectives, which can distract the learners from thinking about what they really need or want to develop.

If a menu system is employed in a work-based, skills-development programme, learners should be assisted to ground their choice by relating it to job demands and current levels of skill.

Beyond the menu system, tutors can help learners to identify their learning needs by a number of means, beginning with ways which do little more than encourage personal reflection and self-analysis, and working up to methods such as assessment centres and individualized learning needs analysis.

Personal reflection and self-analysis

To perform an analysis that is acceptable to the individual, congruent with the principles of the learning contract, and achieved at a reasonable expense, the preferred method is self-diagnostic. This can take the form of a structure, method, or instrument, which the learner is advised or required to use. There are three common types:

- using models of good practice
- self-analysis questionnaires
- obtaining feedback from others.

Models of good practice

Studying a model of good practice can provide the learner with new ideas, benchmarks, points of reference and means of overcoming problems. A realistic model of good practice encourages the personal comparison and evaluation of one's own performance that is at the heart of self-analysis.

Part of the value in studying models of good practice is to build up the learning momentum of people undertaking a development programme. Assistance and guidance in the earlier stages of such a programme appear to be very important. Rather than designing a programme that consists entirely of individualized learning contracts, it seems more effective to concentrate on some standard, established body of knowledge as a first stage. This may be no more than a relevant body of knowledge, or a model of competence, or a number of different perspectives on the role of a learner, or an investigation into a fundamental skill area which requires some self-examination. The benefits of this are:

- it stimulates thought on the part of the learner and encourages exploration and self-examination
- it gives the learner time to become used to the idea of preparing a learning contract proposal.

If there is a group of learners this also acts:

- to give the individuals in the group time to get to know each other and lay the foundations for any support.

This early period of guided activity may provide both priming and needs analysis opportunities, and may create a sense of occasion and general direction resulting in greater motivation to succeed on the programme.

Box 5.1 Models of good practice

Competence models provide the most obvious models of good practice for learners. In the UK in particular, detailed Occupational Standards may be available for the area the learner wishes to target.

With all competence models it is important to take learners through the stages indicated by Boyatzis who, as we saw in Chapter 2, set out a series of stages that learners need to undertake when they work with a competence model, beginning with spending time on recognition and understanding of the model and what the competence behaviours will look like in practice. Many of the Occupational Standards models are comprehensive – that is to say very big and complex – and learners may not find them easy to use right away.

I have found that when using behavioural models of competence, a useful exercise is to encourage learners to picture what the behaviour looks like now, and then to suggest what improvement might look like.

For example, one behaviour in the Boyatzis (1982) model is that the manager:

consistently expresses little ambivalence about decisions that he or she has made.

Possible improvements, suggested by a group of middle managers, include:

- demonstrating a better understanding of both sides of the argument, but remaining unequivocal about the ultimate decision
- less hesitation and better timing in explaining the decisions
- better able to withstand public challenge to decisions
- becomes as confident in explaining decisions to bosses as in explaining them to peers/subordinates.

See also Boak 1991b.

There is unlikely to be a shortage of models for study. Competency models of various kinds have been developed for many work roles in recent years. Depending on the programme, and the roles of the learners, some *occupational standards* may be appropriate models of good practice. There are also a variety of models of *personal effectiveness*, which may be appropriate. For in-company programmes there may be suitable company-specific models.

Of course, models of good practice come in many shapes and forms. They may be taken from published material on the relevant areas, or they may be derived from the experiences of the group of learners. Published models may have more authority – but the most appropriate approach will depend on the circumstances. It can sometimes be effective to take a middle path

Figure 5.1   Using different models at different stages

and have learners work on a published model to amend it, to make it relevant for their circumstances. This can increase learners' understanding and ownership and allows for individual variations, while at the same time providing some form of authoritative base.

Depending on the programme and the parameters of the contract, it may be possible to provide a general model that covers all aspects of good practice. This can enable learners to gain an overview of the whole territory in order to decide where they wish to concentrate their energies. Once they have chosen a particular area, more specific models of good practice may be studied and used to aid their reflection (Figure 5.1).

Models for specific areas are usually best employed after the learner has chosen the contract area, either as a precursor to establishing the terms of the contract or as part of the contract itself. The use of a live role model should not be overlooked in this context. It may be possible for the learner to identify a role model for the skill he/she wishes to develop, and to learn from that person: first by observation, then by reflection on what makes that person a skilled performer, perhaps by interviewing the person and modelling the desired behaviour. The advantages of living models are obvious: they have the potential to make much more of an impact on the learner than reading about principles and techniques. But it is often difficult to make sense of what one sees. The design of the learning contract can help, by guiding the learner's attention towards the particular behaviours of the living model that are associated with the skill to be learned.

Self-analysis questionnaires

Questionnaires are often a helpful way of structuring an audit for a learner.

A model of good practice can be converted into a simple, reflective questionnaire by some re-wording and the provision of a scoring system. This can enable the learner to gain a quick impression of where they feel relatively confident, and where they feel some development is desirable. If they want to check their self-assessment, their scores can be compared with how their colleagues score them, using virtually the same questionnaire.

Another format for the self-analysis questionnaire contains a large number

Box 5.2 Simple reflection questionnaires

The MCI Senior Management Standards (1995) have been used as the basis for a simple reflective questionnaire. The detail of the standards is simplified for first use, and learners are asked to rate themselves against each broad area – as in the example below. This format of questionnaire can also be used to gather feedback from others.

How well do you meet these Standards?

rate 1–9

External Trends:	Monitor and influence external factors	

A good manager is able to:

- identify customer needs
- spot opportunities for product and service development
- gather information on wider political and regulatory factors
- identify and evaluate competitors and collaborators.

of statements about activities, feelings or preferences, and the respondent indicates agreement or disagreement. A de-coding sheet groups the responses into categories, and aggregates scores for each category. At this point a briefing sheet will make clear the identity of the categories and provide guidance on the meaning of the scores. Well-known examples in the management and organization field include the Woodcock and Francis (1996) Blockages Survey, the Belbin Team Roles Questionnaire and the Learning Styles Questionnaire. This is the format of most psychometric tests and many entertaining self-analysis quizzes in magazines.

As an aid to diagnosis prior to undertaking a learning contract, a general questionnaire can be very useful. A more specialized questionnaire may be appropriate when the learner has already chosen a contract area, prior to the contract being agreed, or even as part of the contract, to establish learning priorities. Alternatively, a range of specialized questionnaires may be used to help learners establish where they stand in a number of key areas.

Questionnaires can help the learner to focus attention on development through an analysis of personal strengths and weaknesses. Most questionnaires will show the learner as being strong (scoring well) in some categories and being less strong (scoring badly) in others. The design of the questionnaire sometimes encourages this by creating forced choices between

---

Box 5.3 Coded questionnaires

The Woodcock and Francis Blockages Questionnaire uses 120 questions. Responses are de-coded into twelve categories, including self-management, problem solving skills, creativity and teambuilding capability (Woodcock and Francis 1996).

Of course, any chosen model of competence – a company or industry-wide model, for example – could be adapted to make a questionnaire in this way.

Examples of more specialized questionaires include:

The Learning Styles Inventory, where from responses to 80 statements about behaviour a profile of the individual's approach to learning is mapped against the four categories of Activist, Reflector, Theorist, Pragmatist. This is very suitable in the context of a training or development programme (Honey and Mumford 1982).

A development of this is the Learning Diagnostive Questionnaire, which aims to help people match their knowledge and skills, their attitudes and emotions and the learning opportunities available to them at work (Honey and Mumford 1989).

The Management Team Inventory enables the respondent to map a personal profile of preferred approaches to teamwork (Belbin 1981 and 1993).

---

statements. In other cases, where it is technically possible to score the maximum in each category, it is psychologically unlikely.

There are many advantages of using self-analysis questionnaires as an aid to diagnosis, but there are also a number of potential drawbacks.

1. *Limited categorization*: all questionnaires produce results against pre-defined categories. This can lead to an incomplete picture of what an individual's learning needs are or might be. Simple reflective questionnaires can give the learner the choice of adding other areas for development.

2. *Accurate categorization*: it is not always clear, even with sophisticated and well-tried questionnaires of the coded variety, why a certain response to a certain question should indicate, say, a deficiency in a particular category of skills. Perhaps this is related in some cases to the following point.

3. *Isolation from the job*: by themselves, the results of the questionnaire are at least one step removed from the learner's real development needs – which are linked to current or future job demands. Development needs

---

Box 5.4 Unclear connections

Coded self-analysis questionnaires often make an association between having a liking for an activity and possessing the necessary skills to do it properly, and the reverse: if I dislike an activity, this is symptomatic of a lack of skill. Preferences of this sort may indeed point to shortfalls in performance, but initially they indicate attitudes: I may like a particular activity because of its relative novelty and because I delude myself as to my level of expertise. I may dislike an activity because I have to do it all the time and I find the exercise of the skill tedious, although I am quite a proficient performer.

Sometimes the jumps between question and diagnosis are greater: one psychometric test, for example, gives the respondent the choice between living in a social suburb, or in a deep dark wood, or 'in between'. The sociable suburb and 'in between' count towards an outgoing aspect of personality, and ultimately to a score on the Extraversion scale, although many introverts may enjoy access to society (Rowe 1988).

---

indicated by the first results of the questionnaire may be inappropriate in the context of the job, while particular working practices may distort the answers to the questionnaire.

4. *Accurate self-perception*: one problem with self-analysis questionnaires is the degree to which people are able to assess themselves with accuracy, even if they wish to do so. The simple, reflective tests are most vulnerable to motivational distortion, in that an individual may paint a self-image prettier than true life: the more complex coded tests, which guard against this, need to be de-coded by someone else.

5. *Lack of ownership*: the use of a coded test is the use of a mechanism to which the individual must, to some degree, surrender. After a series of responses to statements of varying relevance, making choices on the basis of inadequate information when in real life the decision would depend upon factors not mentioned in the questionnaire, and deciding between alternatives that may appear equally uninteresting, the individual stumbles through an unfamiliar scoring mechanism to find that he/she has serious problems in an essential skill area. It can be easy to disown these results.

The potential problems of self-analysis questionnaires in this context can be avoided or minimized by:

- careful choice and thorough exploration of the questionnaire by the tutor prior to use

- emphasis on the role of the questionnaire as a tool to assist learning needs analysis – not as a final arbiter of strengths and weaknesses
- encouraging learners to consider the results in relation to their job, or in relation to areas for development they had already considered
- encouraging, where appropriate, learners to discuss results with other people.

As a general rule, if a self-analysis questionnaire is a part of the needs analysis system, some time should be made available for learners to discuss the results – with fellow learners, with their boss or with colleagues – and a tutor should be on hand to answer any queries and to encourage people to see the results in a positive perspective.

Feedback from others

A good means of assessing strengths and weaknesses is for the learners to elicit the opinions of people around them. In the context of work-based learning, the people to survey are work colleagues and the immediate boss. If the learning programme is group-based it may be appropriate to seek feedback from colleagues within the group about behaviour displayed in that context.

If a performance appraisal system operates inside the organization, the learner may receive some information as a matter of course on areas in which he/she should improve. In other cases, it will be necessary for the learner to take the initiative.

Seeking all round – or 360 degree – feedback has become a popular pre-occupation in some areas of the training and development profession (Thatcher 1996; Ashridge 1996; Edwards and Ewen 1996). Feedback is sought from a variety of sources who interact with the learner in the course of his or her work, and who can provide comments on different aspects of his/her performance. Compared with the traditional source of feedback – the individual's immediate boss – the potential benefits are that a more accurate and complete picture is obtained, because information is gathered from the people in the best position to comment on an individual's performance. Who is better placed to evaluate a person's ability to work as part of a team, than the other members of the team? Or to give feedback on an individual's skill in leading constructive committee meetings than fellow members of the committee? Looking for this more complete picture is perhaps particularly advantageous for learners in more senior positions, who may not work at all closely with their immediate boss.

Self-assessment and assessment by the boss are normally included in a 360 degree exercise, but also included may be colleagues, members of the learner's immediate team, other more junior members of staff, customers and suppliers – any of the range of people who work with the learner. It is

---

Box 5.5 I can explain

Where people are asked to distribute feedback questionnaires to colleagues, there can be a tendency to discount some of the feedback, particularly if there are discrepancies between different raters. Examples of reasons for discounting feedback can include:

'That person doesn't see me when I am using that skill'
'This relates to a particular incident'
'I don't think they understood the question'

This is quite common. The Center for Creative Leadership has produced a long list of reasons people have heard for discounting feedback (Lombardo and Eichinger 1989, 1991; see also Kaplan 1991, Chapter 2).

When they are not called upon to comment on every discrepancy, however, learners often do make use of the feedback they have received, focusing on areas of personal concern.

This links to the observations of Smith (1982) that adult learners may choose to take action to improve personal limitations when they are able to make decisions to do so, without pressure from others.

The moral of the experience seems to be that information gained in this way must be treated with caution. Either the majority of decisions about how it will be used should be left with the individual or much carefully directed effort is needed to disentangle the genuine from the phoney reasons for discounting critical feedback.

---

usual for the respondents to be able to give feedback anonymously – which is thought to make them more likely to be honest in their comments. The respondents are usually chosen by the learner, or by the learner in negotiation with a tutor. The results may be interpreted by the learner alone, or discussed in detail with the tutor, depending on the scheme.

The feedback can provide a firm basis for personal development plans. Responses from others sometimes confirm, wholly or partially, an individual's own impressions of their strengths and weaknesses. This confirmation can add impetus to the resolve to work on what are agreed to be the areas that need development.

Where the responses show a consensus about the profile of strengths and weaknesses, the weight of numbers can overcome the learner's suspicions of individual bias which can sometimes prevent acceptance of feedback from the immediate boss. Although denial is still a factor in 360 degree feedback, it is less easy to deny a message that is coming from all points of the compass than a message that comes from one source alone.

Tutors who propose to encourage (or require) learners to seek feedback from others should be aware of the potential barriers.

- The learner may feel uneasy and unsure how to go about approaching people for this feedback.
- Those approached may feel equally uneasy and unsure, and may fudge the issue of pointing to weaknesses.

At the same time the potential advantages (accurate feedback economically obtained) are considerable. There is much that can be done to smooth progress towards these advantages. The tutor can:

- Provide a questionnaire for the learner to give others. The provision of a format will help people structure their feedback. The instrument should be evaluated carefully by the tutor, to minimize the risks of accidentally distorting the results, asking the respondents inappropriate questions, or questions they may not understand. The format can, in addition, include guidance to the respondent to encourage an honest response.
- Discuss the advantages and difficulties of seeking feedback with the learners, allow feelings to surface, and develop an agreed action plan. This discussion can include an acknowledgement of the mixed feelings experienced by people who are in receipt of honest feedback.
- Where applicable, brief the boss of each learner on the programme, explaining the role of feedback in the development process, and thereby encouraging honest, positive responses.

It is preferable to treat the feedback obtained as helpful and supportive of the business of needs analysis, as information the learner can use in making his/her decision, rather than regarding the learner as being bound by the opinions of others.

Individual needs analysis

An individual training needs analysis carried out by the tutor can be an alternative to the self-directed approaches we have considered so far. It may provide certain advantages: as an outsider, the tutor may be able to take a more objective, dispassionate view of the learner's performance; as an expert the tutor can see where things are not working as they should, and can prescribe a remedy. This role of training needs analyst is expensive, however, for the tutor needs to spend time with an individual – observing and discussing, learning the singularities of the individual's job, perhaps interviewing or surveying others – to ensure an accurate as well as an objective and dispassionate diagnosis.

We have seen that the motivation of ownership and responsibility is a

---

Box 5.6 In search of honesty

A format to encourage a direct and honest response might read like this:

'It is difficult to be objective about yourself, or to see yourself as others see you. People can waste a lot of time and energy trying to improve upon what they do in areas where they have no need to improve, and remain unaware of their real development needs.'

'Please help me by answering the questions on the next page honestly and accurately. By doing this you will help me to decide where I should be spending time and effort, and where I should be satisfied with how I am doing right now.'

---

powerful engine, driving the individual to succeed in tackling a learning contract. If the tutor diagnoses certain learning needs it is important that the learner genuinely accepts the need for improvement in these areas before a learning contract is undertaken. The time taken to gain this genuine acceptance should not be underestimated, and this adds to the cost.

Short of a full training needs analysis, there may be scope for greater involvement of the tutor at this stage – as one of the providers of feedback, perhaps, or as an interpreter of feedback received from others. Depending on the programme, there may be scope for an early discussion of the learner's analysis of their own needs, prior to negotiation of the contract.

One possible intervention by the tutor at this stage is to carry out a full needs analysis interview, using a Behavioural Event approach, which can result in a profile of skills and competences of the interviewee.

Assessment centres

The increasing popularity of assessment centres as a means of establishing a profile of individual abilities represents an attempt to attain a rigorous analysis of development needs at a reasonable cost. Assessment centres (sometimes deliberately titled 'development centres' to avoid what are seen as the negative and summative connotations of 'assessment') usually contain a simulation, or a number of simulations and exercises, to allow participants to display a range of abilities. Participants are closely observed and their behaviour is assessed against a model of skills or competences. Feedback is subsequently given to participants on the profile of competences they have displayed.

The champions of assessment centres claim a high degree of accuracy and success for this method (Thornton and Byham 1982) and certainly it can

---

Box 5.7 Behavioural Event interviews

The techniques of Behavioural Event interviewing (BEI) were developed in the United States during the 1970s from Flanagan's Critical Incident method.

George Klemp and David McClelland (1986) write that the BEI tries to:

> get a full report of a specific past occurrence, with a beginning, a middle and an end, and with characters who wanted certain things, thought in certain ways, and acted in certain ways. What the interviewer is trained to avoid is getting generalisations about what the person usually does in typical situations. The reason is that everyone has ideas about what he or she does, and when and why, but these ideas are based partly on theories about the job, so they do not tell much about the person's actual behaviour. By obtaining raw data on the person's behaviour, the behavioural interview [allows] us to get beneath the theories to the specific thoughts and actions that contribute to on-the-job success.

The key principle of BEI is that it seeks and evaluates only evidence of the individual's behaviour. The rule is that statements can only be taken into account, or 'coded', if they are about specific behaviours of the interviewee on a particular occasion, and they are described in sufficient detail for the thoughts, words and deeds to be clear.

Behavioural Event interviews can be used for researching competency models, for recruitment interviewing and for establishing development needs.

---

provide a means of direct observation of behaviour that might be difficult to achieve in the workplace, but it consumes large quantities of tutors' time in preparation of an effective simulation, in implementation of the assessment centre, and delivering the feedback.

Combinations

It should be clear that any method of needs analysis may use a combination of the means described so far, and the right combination will be the one that best fits local conditions. Extensive needs analysis might include 360 degree feedback, and an assessment centre, and a Behavioural Event interview. Minimal needs analysis may comprise simply some discussions of models of good practice. Whatever system we use, we will be operating within given limits of cost, and accuracy, and the learner's acceptance of the results.

Needs analysis may also form part of the contract itself. A problem for learners is that often they don't know what they don't know: they may be aware of a development need in a broad area, but they are unable to be more specific about their desired learning objectives. It may be that in such cases part of the contract will involve further needs analysis, and a specification of clear target areas for development. We shall see examples of this approach in the next chapter.

Review

Some form of learning needs analysis is an important component of programmes that aim to develop skills and competences. In this chapter we have discussed a range of possible approaches, from the minimal model, to the provision of more extensive feedback and evaluation to individuals.

Effective systems of needs analysis will save time, and are likely to increase the learner's commitment at the next stage of the process, the negotiation of the contract – which is the subject of the following chapter.

Chapter 6

First steps in negotiation

This chapter provides a foundation for understanding the effective negotiation of learning contracts. There are some basic principles that distinguish effective contracts from ineffective ones, and good contract negotiations from discussions that end in failure, which we will consider, together with an outline of the role and the skills of the tutor. A brief survey of common problems, and suggestions on how to deal with them, completes the chapter. Chapters 7, 8 and 9 are also about aspects of negotiation; they build on material discussed in this chapter. Ideas on defining assessment measures for learning contracts are discussed in Chapter 8.

The word 'negotiation' is used in a variety of contexts, including international diplomacy, industrial relations collective bargaining, professional contract sales, house purchases, and here, in connection with learning contracts. In some of these contexts there are connotations of hard-nosed characters attempting to get the better of one another, and being less than honest in some of the things they say: in my experience this is not generally characteristic of the negotiation of learning contracts. Here negotiation means two people (or more) reaching agreement about the details of a programme of learning and development. There is some give and take: each person usually has something to contribute to the discussion. Sometimes there is bargaining – about the size of the contract, for example, or the resources it will need, or the exact nature of the assessment. But it is generally a good-natured discussion.

Learners brings to it their wants, and needs, and often some valuable experience. Tutors bring to it their skills – in the subject area and also in the use of learning contracts. They may also bring (and the learner may also expect) resources and support to help the learner complete the contract (Figure 6.1).

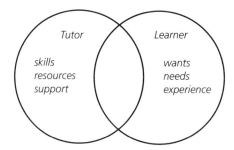

Figure 6.1   Contributing to the contract

Effective negotiation

In sitting down to negotiate a learning contract with a learner, a tutor's aims should be to agree a learning contract that is:

- realistic
- precise and clear
- owned by the learner
- within the rules of the particular scheme.

An effective negotiation achieves this. Sometimes it is a very easy matter, and sometimes unbelievably complicated.

Realism

A realistic contract is one that sets the objectives and the assessments at the right level. The best objectives are achievable, but will involve some stretch on the part of the learner. Realistic objectives are reached through questions that establish the learner's initial level of knowledge and skill, and then gauge the time and application available against potential learning. A realistic contract in this respect is one that challenges, but does not conquer.

The finer points of what constitutes a realistic level of achievement are established by the assessment measures, so in that sense realism is an acute assessment problem and we shall return to it again in the appropriate chapter.

There is a fundamental enemy of realism, however, against which the tutor must guard from an early stage, and that is the dependency. Dependencies are the things the learner is relying on to fulfil the learning contract. They come to light in the course of the action plan and include:

- the person in the other department who will give some information or assistance necessary to complete the contract

- the additional training course where the learner will acquire the basic knowledge necessary for the contract
- the recruitment interview where the targeted interviewing skills will be developed.

And so on.

The dependency can only be flushed out by careful questioning. Learners can be unduly optimistic – reckless even – about what will work out for them.

Precise and clear

The tutor should ensure that the written agreement accurately reflects what the learner aims to learn, and how that learning will be measured, and that the parties to the agreement have a common understanding of what will be done. A part of the process in negotiating a learning contract is to go over what has been written, to question and explain, and make sure the same words mean the same things to different people.

For learning contract formats with a Goal Statement, Learning Objectives and Assessment Measures, there are levels of gradual increasing precision and clarity. Broad statements are acceptable Goals, but more definition is necessary at Objective level and detailed points are advisable for Assessment. This is not difficult where the learning area is naturally amenable to clear delineation, but in other areas it can be more problematic.

A popular acronym for precise and clear objectives is SMART, which is meant to remind us that objectives should be

Specific
Measurable
Achievable
Relevant
Time-bound

In a work environment, *measurable* usually means quantifiable, and *relevant* means that individual objectives are congruent with the objectives of the individual's section, department, company. It is not always feasible to apply sensible quantitative measures to the outcomes of learning contracts, but it can be useful to apply them to places in action plans (how many interviews will the learner carry out? how many questionnaires will they distribute?) and to parts of the assessment measures (how many words will the report contain? how many pieces of feedback will the learner provide?). A completely SMART proposal may not be possible (or even particularly desirable) but proposals can often be made SMARTer in the process of discussion and agreement.

Box 6.1 Dependencies

Eileen saw a major learning opportunity within her own office. A new desk-top publishing system was due to be installed. As office manager, Eileen would need to learn how to use it and then train the remaining office staff. Installation was due the week after this learning contract was agreed, and the first tests of the software would begin at once. Eileen would be able to begin learning how to use the equipment within two weeks.

Of course, installation was delayed, the software proved problematic, and the learning contract suffered a serious set-back because of this.

Another learner, Colin, aimed to improve his counselling/training skills by working with a supervisor who had difficulties with his self-confidence and with his ability to run team briefing meetings. The contract specified that Colin would work with the man for two months, and observe and coach him through four team briefing meetings. After the learning contract had been under way for a month the supervisor was transferred to another section of the department in an apparently unrelated move.

Another learner, Graham, wanted to develop certain leadership competencies, particularly the strategic vision needed to align change projects with relevant strategies and values within an organization. He designed a contract which was based on activities he would carry out in a particular change project he hoped to lead within his company. However, leadership of the project was allocated to someone else, and Graham had to seek another vehicle for his development.

In each of these cases the learning contract was delayed or frustrated by an unforeseen change in the circumstances, in particular a change to a factor on which the contract was dependent. It is not possible to take account of all of these. In particular, cases like Colin's can rarely be foreseen or avoided. In Graham's case the dependency was noted, but the opportunity presented by the project seemed so promising it was decided to wait to see if he would be appointed to lead the team. Eileen's experience is a typical example of dependencies, and similar cases should be thoroughly probed and contingency plans established: this is particularly so when dealing with information technology. The machines never arrive on schedule. There are always problems with the software.

Ownership

It is a fundamental principle of the learning contract approach that the learner should own the contract.

Ownership of the learning contract gives rise to more commitment to seeing it through, overcoming obstacles and achieving its targets.

Ownership means that the contract area has originated with the learner and that he/she has set out, or participated in setting out, the objectives, the action plan and resources needed, and the performance measures. Throughout the process of establishing the learning contract, it is good practice for the learner to initiate proposals, exercise choice between alternatives, and accept or reject suggestions from the tutor.

The tutor may be tempted to take control of the contract for a number of reasons – through inexperience, because he/she feels more comfortable in a telling, directing role, through frustration with the learner's inability to make a decision or take the initiative. Usually they should resist this temptation.

Of course, tutors also often have things of value to add – including important suggestions and recommendations. The role is not entirely a passive one. The value of the suggestion and the recommendation needs to be balanced with the need for the learner to feel ownership.

The rules of the scheme

The contract also needs to meet the rules of the particular scheme, whatever they are. There will be parameters on the possible content of the contract, and probably also on the length of time available for it. And if, for example, regulations require a written report of a certain length, then each contract must include a written report as part of its assessment measures.

Summary

It is obvious that there are potential conflicts here. A tutor can sit down with a learner and draw up a contract that meets three out of these four criteria – but which is not owned by the learner. In order to manage the conflicts that arise, and to ensure that the learner feels ownership of the contract, the tutor may sometimes agree to a contract proposal that is less than technically perfect. In particular, it may be less clear and precise than is ideal; the tutor may also have doubts about the realism of some parts of a proposal, but may have to accept the reassurances of the learner.

A meeting of minds

The process of negotiating the contract varies from scheme to scheme. With short, relatively simple contracts it may take place in one meeting between

---

Box 6.2 Owning the contract

Examples of general rules on ownership are:

- the learner is required to take the initiative in devising the learning contract
- the learner chooses the learning area
- the learner must agree about how and when the learning contract will be assessed
- the agreement is made between a tutor and a learner.

These rules may be subject to constraints in particular schemes, such as:

- regulations may impose limits on the size of the learning contract and the length of time it will take to complete
- the choice of area may be limited to a certain range
- the format of the assessment may be limited to certain types.

---

the tutor and the learner, lasting about an hour, and resulting in a one-page written agreement. Ideally the learner will bring a written proposal, which may be amended in the course of the discussion. At the end of the meeting a copy is made for both parties.

With longer, more complex contracts there may be several meetings, as well as communication by phone, fax and mail before the agreed document is produced. Amendments may be made by word-processor. But there is still likely to be a key meeting (or more than one) where the learner presents his or her proposal and the broad areas to be covered by the contract are agreed.

Before this meeting, whether the contract is simple or complex, certain things should have happened:

- the learner should have been primed about his/her role in the learning contract process
- and should have had enough time to consider a suitable learning area and objectives
- the learner should have had some notice of the meeting, to bring the issues fresh to mind
- and should know how long the meeting will last.

The same applies to anyone else at the meeting. In work-based programmes, for example, it is common to involve a representative from the employer, such as the learner's boss. It may be that the latter will need to be briefed at the start of the meeting, but this allows them very little time to consider what they can contribute, and some briefing should be carried out before this point if at all possible. There is more discussion on this point in Chapter 12.

If all the preliminary and preparatory processes have been carried out properly, the learner should come forward with a clear, realistic contract proposal. With some minor amendments and clarifications it should be agreed and either begun, or work commenced on the detailed drafting. Trouble-free negotiations of this sort do take place, but there are common problems at the negotiation stage, and a section later in this chapter addresses them.

As the tutor, your general approach should be a questioning one. You want to know what the learner proposes to learn. You may need to be patient and wait while the learner presents the background to the proposal. You want to know why the learner has chosen this contract area. You may need to ask this question in a number of different ways to get a clear picture of their motivation. You want to know how the learner proposes to undertake the learning, and when they expect to have achieved their objectives, and what they propose to produce to show that the contract is complete.

A logical sequence is to set out the goal, develop the learning objectives, then develop the action plan and finally set out the assessment measures. The detailed assessment measures are in fact usually the last item to be specified, but the discussion of the contract may begin with the goal, or with the learning objectives, or with action that the learner will undertake.

Work-based learning contracts are particularly likely to begin with a discussion of action, as learners are often aware of actions they are expected to undertake at work during the period of the contract, which represent opportunities or problems, and which they wish to use as vehicles for learning. They may be less clear about the exact nature of the learning they will achieve, and so discussion of the contract begins with an explanation of the work-related actions, and then moves on to consider a range of possible learning goals and objectives.

If the needs analysis part of the preparation for the contract is not highly structured to guide the learner towards a competency or skill model, then the tendency to begin with work-related action is likely to be more pronounced.

In more academic programmes, where the contract method is being used to define an area for research, learners appear more likely to begin with goals and work their way logically through the contract proposal. However, they may be tempted to begin with actions if, for example, they see a good opportunity to gather data from an organization or a pool of respondents: they may start from the premise that they will use this opportunity and then consider a number of different possible specific learning objectives. In fact, many excellent contracts have begun with a consideration of action and opportunity and then worked their way on to a definition of objectives. If this is where the learner wants to start, the tutor is best advised to follow this approach. Sooner or later, however, the learner will have to define their learning objectives, and the tutor may need to prod and probe and make sure that the learner is not thinking exclusively about action and activity, but is also committed to learning. There is more on this, and on the connection between learning contracts and work projects, in the following chapter.

Throughout the discussion of the contract proposal, the tutor spends time:

1. Checking the learner's proposal: reading what has been written and often asking for further explanation in order to ensure a common understanding.

2. Checking the situation: asking about the background to the contract, why the learner has chosen it; often asking for more details on the resources the learner will need, the opportunities they have available, checking on other demands on their time.

3. Suggesting alternatives to the learner's proposals: these may be simple clarifications, to make sure the proposal is precise and clear, or they may be additions to or subtractions from the original proposal. Sometimes it makes sense to suggest a scaling down of a proposal in order to ensure the learner focuses their energy and time on higher-value areas of the contract, or to maintain equity of size of contract with that of other learners on the programme.

The key skills an effective tutor needs at this stage can be summarized briefly as the ability to:

*   gather information
*   provoke reflection
*   summarize and check understanding
*   make suggestions and recommendations
*   remind learners of principles and parameters
*   provide encouragement.

There is more discussion of these skills in Chapter 9.

Common problems

A number of common problems arise when a tutor meets with a learner to agree a contract proposal. Forewarned is forearmed, so this section reviews some of these problems and suggests actions a tutor can take.

1. The unprepared learner

The priming and needs analysis process may have failed, and the learner arrives at the negotiation with no proposal to make. This tends to indicate lack of commitment or organization.

The tutor's options are:

- to attempt to establish, from this 'cold start', a learning area or a development need the learner might address, and then draw up a learning contract.

This is only feasible at all with short contracts, and in any case it is hard work and is unlikely to produce a learning contract to which the learner feels committed. Alternatives are:

- to attempt to draw out from the learner any areas they have considered for the contract, to discuss how they might carry out some further analysis of their aims or needs, and arrange to meet to agree the learning contract at a later date
- to re-state the basic rule, that the learner is responsible for making a proposal, and cut the discussion short.

The choice will depend on the tutor, the learner, and the aims of the scheme. Discussing possible contract areas and making a second appointment may be the best option if this is the learner's first contract, or if the contract is in a completely new area. If the dependent or disorganized behaviour pattern recurs, however, the third option may be the one which will best reinforce the message about the learner's responsibility.

Sometimes a learner may present a choice between a number of different learning contracts. If this is the first contract the learner and tutor have met to discuss, the learner might express some concern about whether a contract of a particular type, or in a certain area, will be acceptable. If all of the options are acceptable it is arguably advisable for the tutor to push the choice back to the learner, to emphasize where the responsibility lies. This may take time and patience: in fact, one of the major problems of encountering unprepared learners is the unanticipated and unscheduled length of the discussion which ensues.

2. The uncertain learner

A difficulty for people approaching a learning contract can be that they don't know what they don't know – in particular they may be unaware of the ideas and the language they need to structure their contract proposal. A common approach, therefore, is for learners to talk about a broad area, or to raise a problem.

If the learner proposes a broad area, the tutor's best approach is to try to

---

Box 6.3 Helping the uncertain learner

Where a learner wants to develop some aspect of a skill, but has insufficient knowledge about the skill, or about which area in particular that they need to develop, the natural first steps are for them to remedy these two areas of uncertainty. It is sometimes appropriate to include these processes of discovery and self-analysis as part of the contract; in other situations it may be better to specify them as activities that must be undertaken before the contract is agreed.

Using this approach the learner:

- acquires knowledge of good practice, perhaps by reading recommended books, studying recommended models or discussing the matter with a skilled performer. From this a model is developed which defines the skill area. This model, which represents the learner's acquired understanding, forms part of the assessment of the contract
- compares their own performance with the good practice defined in the model and establishes priorities for development
- concentrates on a (specified) limited number of learning priorities, and looks to make progress against them over a fixed period of time
- evaluates progress and sets out an action plan for further development.

---

break it down into its constituent parts, and to elicit a more precise description of what it entails. This may mean, for example, asking why a learner has chosen this as a contract area. In a skills development contract it may mean asking what particular kinds of things the learner wants to be able to do better.

For skills development contracts, further analysis and self-analysis might be needed. Depending on the programme and the parameters of the contract, this may be something that could be included as part of the contract or the contract might be delayed until this diagnostic work has been carried out.

The tutor has a choice here, between trying to establish, through questioning, the most relevant aspect of the skill area to the learner or, alternatively, suggesting an action plan and objectives that lead the learner to acquire a knowledge base across the whole area.

3. The ambiguous proposal

Where the wording of the contract proposal is ambiguous, different perceptions of the learning contract may arise, which can lead to problems. This ambiguity may be obvious at the time, if the aims of the contract are defined in very broad or vague terms, but it may be less apparent. The learner who

Box 6.4 Helping the uncertain learner 2

It may be possible in the course of discussion to establish the learner's aims and their current level of knowledge and skill: for example, Rob wanted to 'learn something about computers'.

The tutor asked questions such as: what aspect of computing do you most want to know about? What experience of computing have you had so far?

At one point the tutor suggested: perhaps the first thing is to have a clear idea of what the area involves. The three most common computing programmes are spreadsheets, databases and word-processing. How about we say you'll be able to explain what each of them can do as your first objective?

After discussion about relevance to his job, however, and his current level of knowledge (minimal) it was agreed that he would learn how to use a database package in an area of practical use to his job.

The assessment measures, proposed by the tutor, were that he would produce a database application that he created, using a standard package, with at least eight fields, and be able to access data through at least four of these, and at least twenty files. He would be able to demonstrate that he could input new data, amend errors to data and access data as requested by the assessor.

In designing the assessment, as in this case, the tutor becomes more of a leader, a teller, an owner of the contract and the learner becomes more of a follower, a person who is told, and less of an owner of the contract. This is perhaps inevitable where the learner knows little about the area of skill or knowledge targeted in the contract. The tutor should *suggest* or *propose* rather than direct, and seek to give the learner choices.

Of course, the tutor needs to know enough about the area to specify the parameters of the knowledge base. If not then a specialist needs to be brought in to the discussion.

Information technology is an area where it is possible to quantify and be precise about targets, and where demonstration of the acquired skills can be specified in the assessment.

proposes, in one line of their action plan, to 'issue a questionnaire to staff', may have a very different picture of what this entails, and the amount of time it will take, to that of the tutor. At one extreme, the questionnaire might be a simple one-page sheet requiring yes/no responses distributed to three work colleagues. At the other extreme it could be three pages of questions that invite graded and descriptive answers, sent out to twenty people.

Reading 'relevant literature' can be a common ambiguous proposition; including the booklist for the entire module is only slightly more definite. Some checking here on the learner's actual plans can usually determine whether beneath this vague description there is a realistic and acceptable plan, or whether the underlying intentions are in fact equally vague.

Presenting 'a report' is a common proposal for an assessment point. The tutor who fails to discuss and agree some features of this report – such as a summary of content or chapter heading, and approximate length – may often encounter problems at a later stage.

A detailed draft learning contract proposal indicates enthusiasm and commitment. A good general rule, to leave ownership with the learner and to avoid dismotivation, is to make the minimum number of amendments necessary. In the case of minor amendments, best practice is to clarify the assessment measures – usually to make them more specific. While other aspects of the learning contract may be less than ideal in a technical sense, it is often better to let them pass and retain the learner's motivation, as long as the assessment is precise and realistic.

4. The unrealistic proposal

A different kind of problem occurs when the learner presents a proposal that appears to involve more time and effort than is practicable, or access to information or resources that will not be available. The learner may be too ambitious. This can cause a dilemma for tutors who do not wish to dampen enthusiasm or discourage the sense of ownership and responsibility which ambitious and optimistic learners often feel for their proposals.

We have already described some aspects of achieving a realistic contract, earlier in this chapter. A key role for the tutor is to check on dependencies in the learner's proposal. A good way to do this is to check the learner's reasoning, and to get them to think about the details of their plan of action: how do they know they will be able to gain access to the information they want? What will they do if they can't access the information? When will they know if the information will be available?

If the contract seems over-ambitious because the learner is promising to do too many things, the best approach for the tutor is to check what the learner sees as the main focus or purpose of the proposal. Some parts of the proposal may be peripheral to the main aim. It generally does no harm for the tutor to reflect on the apparent large scale of the contract to the learner. The learner may then agree to drop some of the peripheral aspects of the proposal from the contract.

Sometimes an ambitious and optimistic proposal accompanies a rather cavalier attitude to the contents of the contract. The tutor may help the learner to think more realistically by pointing out that if an objective is included in the contract then it must be achieved, if an action is proposed then it must be carried out, and the learner must be able to show that they can meet all (not just some of) the assessment measures they propose.

5. The lightweight proposal

At the other end of the scale, some learners may put forward proposals that appear too limited and unambitious. With adult learners on management development programmes I have rarely found this to be a problem: perhaps one contract in twenty falls into this category, compared with perhaps six or seven that are over-ambitious and need to be scaled down.

As the tutor your first step is to check on your understanding of the proposal: what may at first glance seem unambitious may in fact be very difficult. If, after checking, the proposal still seems to be a little light in substance, remind the learner of the expected scale of the contract (according to the aims and/or the rules of the programme, which will have been communicated during the priming process). It may then be possible to suggest additional activities, assessments, objectives which can be incorporated into the proposal. On academic programmes, for example, this may mean the learner accepting the need for additional ideas and wider reading, or undertaking a little more empirical research than is contained in the original proposal. On skills development programmes it may mean that the learner will go beyond improving their understanding, and undertake more practice, or seek more structured feedback on their practised performance.

If, as the tutor, you suspect that the contract proposal is deliberately scaled down to what the learner thinks they can get away with, you will be well advised to make sure the assessment measures are very precise: pay extra attention to defining and quantifying them. But be aware that a contract proposal may be unambitious more through a sense of trepidation (or lack of confidence) on the part of the learner than any other reason: check and, if appropriate, provide reassurance.

6. The helpless tutor

Sometimes learners may want to undertake a contract in an area the tutor knows little or nothing about. On an academic programme, this may be an arcane area of the subject. On a work-based programme, it may be something to do with the systems and processes within the learner's company. Under these circumstances, it is difficult to help the learner to devise a good contract, and it is difficult to assess the completed piece of work.

There are two possible tactics which you, as the tutor, might employ:

- involve someone who does know about the area
- find out about it yourself.

Box 6.5 The helpless tutor

The tutor's lack of expertise may not prevent him/her assisting in drawing up a contract, although it will limit the role he/she can play in assessment.

For example, in the (relatively few) contracts my colleagues and I negotiated on learning parts of a foreign language, it was possible to agree with the learner what they would learn, and the format in which they would prove this. One learner wanted to be able to speak some basic Arabic (he was going on a secondment to the Middle East). We agreed that he would be able to speak some basic terms, which we specified in English – there were some common pleasantries, some engineering terms, and some numbers. Part of the evidence was a tape recording of him speaking these words, which we arranged to have assessed by a tutor from a language school. There was also a written testimonial from a colleague in the Middle East. A similar contract was devised for someone who wanted to be able to give a lecture in French. (Obviously in these cases it is important to be quite clear in setting out the criteria for success, so that the specialist assessor may use them for guidance.)

In contracts where part of the learning is about company systems and procedures, and how to use them, a local expert (either the learner's line manager or a functional specialist) will be needed for part of the assessment. It can be beneficial to have this expert involved directly in the negotiation of the contract, as they will be able to give a realistic estimate of the difficulty of the contract and the effort needed to complete it. Learning how to make a proposal for capital investment may be very quick and easy, involving little learning, and hardly enough to merit a contract; or it may be very difficult and time-consuming, and probably larger than other contracts that are being undertaken on the programme. The tutor has little way of knowing, without personally finding out about the system.

The need to take the second option on occasions provides some of the great satisfaction – and personal development – for tutors who use learning contracts. It is not always a practical option, of course, and you may need to involve another person in the contract. Depending on the circumstances, this may be another tutor or a specialist contacted by the tutor or by the learner. On work-based programmes there is often a need for someone from within the learner's company to play a role in agreeing and assessing the contract.

Review

This chapter has introduced some of the basic issues relevant to negotiating a learning contract. Negotiations are usually good-natured meetings of minds, where both parties bring valuable contributions to the discussion. The role of the tutor is to help the learner produce a written statement of their intent which is realistic, precise and clear, owned by the learner, and which falls within any rules which apply to the scheme.

Some of the common problems of negotiating learning contracts have been outlined. The following chapter deals with some more difficulties, and suggests strategies for dealing with them.

Chapter 7

Advanced negotiation

Now that we have covered some basic points on negotiating successful learning contracts, this chapter introduces some of the particular difficulties that can be found when:

- using learning contracts to help people to develop skills
- linking learning contracts to work-based projects
- using learning contracts with placements
- agreeing learning contracts with three (or more) people.

Skills development contracts

In Chapter 2 we saw that learning contracts are very well suited to helping people to develop generic and specific skills, and to develop competences. Negotiation of these contracts often poses additional problems for learner and tutor, however, and it is as well to be forewarned of the common pitfalls and opportunities. Some of the problems centre on the difficulties of defining learning objectives in certain skills areas, but there are also problems caused at this stage by inadequate or mistaken needs analysis, and by the reluctance of learners to admit to development needs.

Defining the contract

Unless their scope is constrained by the programme of which they are a constituent part, contract proposals can come in all shapes, sizes and degrees of detail. Learning contracts are potentially able to accommodate skill development in any area the learner wants or needs. These can be strange and wonderful: from learning pieces of foreign languages, to learning how to use computers to gather, analyse, transform and communicate information; from financial or marketing analyses, to the legion of social and interper-

---

Box 7.1 Defining the right skill

A supervisor in a busy factory was concerned that his ability to represent his point of view in meetings was letting him down.
  A contract was agreed whereby he would:

- arrive at a clear picture of the skills required to contribute to meetings – this from reading practical texts and observing colleagues, and then making his own list
- establish his strengths and weaknesses in terms of these skills – this he did by using a scoring system for himself, and also asking his immediate boss to score him
- develop his skills in two target areas.

In this way, he drew on the published ideas of others, and the perceptions of someone close to him.
  Note: this is a specific example of the general shape of this type of contract set out in Box 6.3.

---

sonal skills needed to recruit, motivate, counsel, persuade, lead, discipline, challenge and co-operate with other people.

The point here is a simple one: it is not always possible to be certain in advance what the focus of the learning contract should be. Some learners will present firm and clear proposals – and will produce them in advance if necessary. Others will present more or less clear proposals, but in the course of discussion it will become apparent that the best contract would be elsewhere.

Proposals are likely to arrive in varying degrees of detail. Learner A might have managed to put nothing on paper, but says he wants to do 'something on interview skills'. Learner B may have thought more deeply about what she wishes to learn, and may have broken down a skill area into its component parts, with a means of assessment against each objective. The former proposal often takes a conventional skill area such as making presentations, interviewing, time management or computing. The tutor should establish what the learner means by the expression, and whether he/she can be more precise about the learning objectives. It may be that the tutor's questions will reveal that the learner has a very clear idea of what he/she wants to achieve, in which case all is well. It will also reveal some learners for whom the skill area is a blank box – whether it be about making a presentation, interviewing or computing – and the tutor must decide on a strategy to help the learner define the area.

In the previous chapter we noted that precision in objectives is easier to achieve in some areas than in others. In cases where the learner sets out

Box 7.2 Levels of competency

The excellent dictionary of competencies produced by Spencer and Spencer of McBer and Co. contains examples of definitions of levels of ability which can be used directly in a learning contract, or can provide a clear illustration to learners and tutors of how increasing levels of skill can be defined. Many company-based models that are used in appraisal systems provide a similar key to levels of skill.

In the McBer model, for example, the competency of *Teamwork and Co-operation* is measured on three different dimensions. The primary dimension concerns the thoroughness or intensity of the person's actions to promote teamwork, and is scaled on seven levels. Levels 5, 6 and 7 are:

5. Empowers others: publicly praises others who have performed well. Encourages others and makes them feel strong and important.
6. Teambuilds: promotes a friendly and co-operative climate – organizes group events and parties, creates symbols of group identity. Promotes the group to outsiders.
7. Resolves conflicts: surfaces conflicts within the team and encourages a positive resolution of them.

(Spencer and Spencer 1993)

to improve interpersonal skills, for example, precision and understanding may fly out of the window, and it can be helpful – if a little mechanistic – to break the skill down into component parts as a method of establishing targets.

In Chapter 2 we introduced a visual model of staged improvement as a way of picturing the skills development that a person might achieve in a learning contract. In practice, it is often difficult to define with any clarity the stages of increasing skill that would be represented by each of the steps. Some of the more sophisticated competency models present descriptions of these defined steps, which can be useful (Spencer and Spencer 1993). Often the best that can be done in defining the learning objectives is to set out the area for improvement: greater precision comes in the action plan and the assessment measures.

Where it is difficult to be precise in defining the learning objectives, it is even more important to be as precise as possible in defining the action plan and the performance measures.

Gauging the stretch

The objectives in a learning contract should be realistic – that is, they should be achievable in the contract period. Ideally, they should contain a degree of stretch, so that learners need to apply themselves in order to be successful. If they are part of a qualification programme, equity demands that there should be some degree of equivalence between different contracts. On a qualification programme there may also be issues about a minimum standard of performance that must be reached by the completion of the contract.

Gauging the degree of stretch in a learning contract is partly a matter of making an evaluation of the individual's level of skill at the outset of the contract, and estimating what degree of improvement is realistic over the time period of the contract.

Of course, the visual image of staged improvement, the stairway, shows a more regular progression than is found in reality. Learning curves are seldom so neat. At times, the pace of learning may be faster than envisaged, or it may be much slower as the learner reaches a blockage or a plateau. It is often very difficult to estimate precisely how much improvement an individual will achieve over a given time period. Where this is the case, careful estimates must be made of the possible inputs to the learning process, and these should be specified clearly, as should the outputs from the process, i.e. the assessment measures.

Developing the right skills

Sometimes learners propose broad skill areas and it is necessary to work with them to establish which part of the skill area they really need to develop.

Sometimes learners propose to develop focused skills, but there is a problem in that the proposal is the learner's solution to a particular problem and it is the wrong solution.

An apparently sensible learning contract could be agreed that would result in no skill development (because lack of the skill is not the cause of the performance problem) or disenchantment (because the skill development does not result in resolution of the problem).

It is good practice, therefore, to ask why the learner wants to undertake development of the chosen skill and, if appropriate, to question the diagnosis that points to this skill area as the solution to that problem.

In a classic example of this, a junior manager, Mike, wanted to improve his performance in meetings. Recently he had been embarrassed on more than one occasion in meetings with clients. He presented his contract proposal as one which focused on better preparation for these meetings, and an improvement in his abilities to make formal presentations to customers.

Fortunately, discussion with his line manager during the negotiation of the learning contract cast doubt on the benefit of developing these skills. Mike's line manager agreed that some specific aspects of presentation skills could be improved upon, but that another dimension of the problem concerned self-confidence in discussing matters with customers and more senior managers. After a long discussion, Mike agreed to focus the contract on this aspect of his self-presentation. One of the measures he agreed to undertake was to develop 'scripts' to handle situations he found difficult – which meant changing some of the sentence structures he commonly used.

Preparation and formal presentation skills did not appear in the learning contract. They were low priority – or no priority – learning areas. The contract was very successful in improving his performance.

Learners in Mike's position are normally concerned with a difficulty, a problem or an aggravation, but they are not sure what to do about it. Mike had made a conscientious attempt to specify a solution. ('Better preparation' is often put forward as a solution to interpersonal skills problems – sometimes realistically so.) In some cases, particularly where the needs analysis methods are not particularly systematic, learners outline the problem and look to the tutor for advice, with greater or lesser expectations of a miracle cure. Examples include the learner who wanted more commitment from his team, the learner who wanted to have more impact in meetings, the learners who have suffered from stress or from time pressure problems, the learner who wanted to gain more respect from his colleagues and more credit for the ideas he produced.

The actual skills and the means of developing them may be difficult to define. In some cases this is because the problem has not been well defined, or the causes of the problem have not been identified. The first steps to take with the learner who wants to have more impact in meetings, for example, involve finding out what this means. What meetings? What does he/she want to achieve? How are people reacting to him/her now? How does he/she want them to react?

Sometimes the problem can be accurately identified before the contract is agreed, and its causes narrowed down to a limited range of possibilities. In most learning contracts that begin with a problem, part of the contract is to analyse the problem and the learning priorities. In these cases the model of the learning contract is:

- gather and record information on the problem: when it occurs, what are the symptoms, what are the possible causes
- identify priorities in tackling the problem
- identify techniques or best practices to handle priority areas
- apply techniques over a period of time, and evaluate progress
- specify an action plan for further development.

Establishing possible causes of the problem may require an excursion into theory, or the acquisition of facts or information from colleagues.

The learner is likely to look to the tutor for suggestions as to further

---

Box 7.3 Developing the right skills

Mike's learning contract was:

GOAL

To develop techniques to improve my ability to feel more comfortable and to deal more professionally and confidently with more senior managers and customers.

OBJECTIVES

1. To identify occasions in dealing with other people, particularly senior managers or customers, when I feel comfortable and in control, and occasions when I don't.
2. To have a clear understanding of what I am already doing right and what I could do better in those situations.
3. To improve my ability to handle situations where I currently feel uncomfortable.
4. To understand how to develop further.

ASSESSMENT

1. Analyses of at least six occasions, setting out what happened, what I did right, what I could do better next time, how I felt.
2. Brief written statement and oral explanation of conclusions about what I could do.
3. Review of progress of attempts to use different methods of handling the situations.
4. Brief written statement and oral explanation of remaining immediate barriers.
5. Statement of action plan for further progress.

ACTIVITIES

1. To identify techniques, from reading, that I think I could use.
2. To identify other people who handle 'difficult' situations well and to analyse how they say things and how they respond to pressure.
3. To analyse situations where I deal with seniors and customers; considering points set out in Assessment 1.

---

reading or constructs or methods for gathering and analysing information from others. The proposal that the problem should be tackled using the model outlined above will almost certainly need to come from the tutor.

The presentation of a problem as the starting point for a learning contract can be a genuine and productive approach. It may not be so neatly packaged as a straightforward proposal of a skill area as the target for development, but the effects may be more significant, useful and durable.

Using learning styles

In Chapter 2, we introduced the Learning Cycle, the series of activities that a person must undertake in order to develop a skill: action, reflection, theorizing and planning. It seems apparent that individuals have different preferences for these activities – perhaps strongly preferring one or more of them, and perhaps showing an aversion to one or more of the others (Honey and Mumford 1982). So, the high Activists will prefer to learn skills by throwing themselves into practice, while the high Reflectors will be more anxious to reflect and evaluate; high Theorists will seek out the key principles they should follow, while high Pragmatists will want to set out a workable action plan.

The strengths in the profile are not particularly problematic for the use of learning contracts – but the weaknesses, the areas where an individual shows a low score, may create difficulties.

When using contracts on skill development, it is useful to discuss learning styles, to use the Learning Styles Questionnaire (Honey and Mumford) with learners and to discuss the results. Areas of low preferences can then be reinforced in drawing up the contract:

Low Activists   agree some explicit action that will be taken
Low Reflectors   agree on points or headings that the learner will evaluate
Low Theorists   agree on specific readings or principles that the learner will explore
Low Pragmatists   check out all the details of the learner's proposal very carefully.

Proposals to improve knowledge

Even on a skills development programme, some contract proposals may be framed strongly in terms of knowledge, where the learning objectives are those of acquiring information. The information might be practical and factual (e.g. how the company cost code system works, the correct procedure to follow in routing products to repair, where I am using my time, what the training needs of my staff are) or more theoretical (e.g. methods of prioritizing demands on my time, theories of group behaviour, ideas about origins of stress).

Learners may propose contracts that are biased towards gathering information, because:

- it is easy to define information that one would like to know, or can learn, but it is more difficult to define skills
- it can be more acceptable to admit to not knowing information in a certain area, whereas it may be less acceptable (or more risky) to admit to skills needs.

Where the learner produces a contract proposal that aims to 'find out about' or to 'understand' facts, procedures or processes, it may be possible for the tutor to suggest that the contract also covers other stages of the Learning Cycle. If the original proposal concerns *knowledge*, it may be feasible to move part of the contract towards the preparation of an action plan, and also to taking action in the light of the new knowledge. If the learner agrees, this amendment can be made to the objectives and to the assessment points.

Work-based projects and learning contracts

On work-based learning programmes, there is often confusion between *learning contracts* and *change projects*, which can take hold at the outset of the contract and/or arise during the implementation and assessment of the contract. The distinction between these two approaches to work-based learning are:

- projects are essentially activity-orientated and geared towards producing results in the sense of improvements or changes to working practice
- learning contracts are explicitly focused upon learning, and improvements or changes to personal behaviour.

Examples of a project might include: to introduce new technology into a section of the company; to carry out a feasibility study of an operation to compare the advantages of direct against contract labour; to gain agreement on a policy change or a re-organization; to solve a problem affecting productivity.

Change projects are frequently associated with work-based learning, partly because of their novelty to the learner and the degree of extra challenge they involve (McCall *et al.* 1988).

Discussion of a learning contract proposal may begin with the learner presenting a work-based project. This may be because the learner is faced with a new work challenge and therefore feels that he or she is bound to learn something. The learner may also wish to include the change project within their contract because incorporating it within a learning contract might provide a learning arena of a suitable size.

In some programmes, learning contracts may be specifically linked to change projects, with the change project providing a vehicle for the learning

---

Box 7.4 Losing sight of the learning

Oliver had decided that he needed to develop his ability to explain complex proposals for change clearly and persuasively to others. He was a highly intelligent person, and he had a bad habit of losing his listeners by explaining his proposals at too high a level of complexity, or too quickly.

He chose a large-scale project as the vehicle for this contract. He was senior manager in a multinational company, and he had been charged with investigating how the various management information systems used in the various parts of the company could be aligned with one another.

The project took him around the world, talking to the subsidiary companies in four different continents, and involved him in a great deal of organizational politics. Although the skill he had chosen to develop was crucial to his success in the project, he frequently lost sight of the learning objective of developing this skill as he struggled to achieve success in the project.

This project also provides an example of the difficulties of timing work-based activities with programme demands. Oliver started this contract earlier in the programme than was originally scheduled, to accommodate the start of the project. The work had still not reached a conclusion ten months later, when the contract was assessed, and Oliver provided a summary of his progress on the project 'at time of writing'.

---

and development. The stages of the change project in these cases will form part of the action plan of the learning contract (Mumford 1988, Chapter 2).

However, there is a danger that learners will become distracted from the aims and assessment measures of the learning contract. They may devote all, or the best part, of their energies to achieving the project outcomes and fail to address the learning objectives. This is not unusual.

* The participant (and his/her line manager) may be more concerned with the short-term benefits of project work (action, leading to results) than the longer-term benefit of a learning contract (development, leading to improved ability). This may corrupt the negotiation process.
* Projects have a longer history as components of work-based programmes than learning contracts. The priming operation with the participant (and his/her line manager, if this applies) may have failed and there may be genuine misunderstanding about what is required.

Where a learner concentrates on the project, on action, on results in the workplace, the tutor needs to draw them back to learning and development. This may be necessary at the outset, in negotiating the contract; it may become necessary again as the contract progresses; and even at the conclusion of the contract, the learner may need to be prompted to reflect on and demonstrate the targeted learning. The drift of the learner's focus from the contract to the project, from development to achievement, can take place even when there is a relatively thorough priming and needs analysis system, particularly if the project is a challenging one.

At the negotiation stage, there are two common problems exhibited by learners who are thinking too much about the project and not enough about the learning contract.

1. The learner presents activities or work outcomes as learning objectives.

As anyone who has applied the Task, Knowledge, Skills, Attitude format of job analysis knows, there can be initial difficulties in distinguishing between doing something (task) and the ability to do it (skill). This is a particular problem when the social nature of the task means that demonstration of the skill by repeated performance of the task (as in information technology skills, or financial analysis skills) is not possible.

The tutor here needs to point out the difference between learning objectives and task objectives, and to remind the learner that the contract is about learning and development. A useful strategy is to persist with the question: 'What will you learn by doing this?'

2. The learner includes a list of skills or competences that will be called upon in the course of the project and includes them as learning objectives, defined in broad terms. Request for further definition will usually lead to additions to this list, still defined in broad terms.

This is not helpful in defining a learning contract. The statements are usually too broad to form objectives or to be assessed; typically they represent a contract that is too large.

The best strategy for the tutor is to point out the difficulties of the broad descriptions, and the size of the contract, and to try to establish the learner's development priorities between the skill areas he or she has put forward, before trying to reach a more precise definition of the area that is most important to him or her.

A final issue with linking work-based projects to learning contracts can be difficulties over timing. Progress on the work-based project will be dependent on various factors in the workplace. The schedule may be accelerated, or the project may be delayed, or aborted, in contradiction to the learner's expectations at the outset. Matching the schedule of a learning contract and a development programme to the quite different schedule of a company's immediate needs for results and achievement is not always a simple task. Learners should be supplied with all the information they need to be able to plan ahead, and the programme schedule may need to be treated with some flexibility to accommodate the timing of events in the workplace.

Box 7.5 The list of skills

Linda presented the following proposal for a learning contract:

Goal. To plan, organize, market and run a training course for [clerical and reception staff within the department] on customer care skills.
  Note that this is a project goal, not a learning contract goal.

Objectives

1. Development of training skills.
2. Marketing knowledge and practice.
3. Expansion of planning skills.
4. Knowledge of publicity and advertising.

The assessment proposals were similarly lacking in detail, and heavily reliant on evaluations carried out by others.
  Of the two groups of skills – training and marketing – Linda thought that the training skills would generally be employed and developed the most. The learning contract was amended to focus on planning and design skills (assessed through a log and a statement of learning objectives) and actual delivery skills (Linda to identify and describe them, and to receive feedback on her performance).
  The marketing element was specified as an understanding of the market for the course, why this market might attend and how they might be contacted. This omits much of the very broad area of marketing, but it was what was relevant to Linda.

Learning contracts and placements

Learning contracts are sometimes seen as ideal ways of structuring learning on placements or secondments (Laycock and Stephenson 1993, Section 3). In theory, a firm written agreement, specifying particular target areas for learning, will help a person in such a situation get the most from the new experience. In practice, their effectiveness appears to depend on:

- the extent to which the demands of the placement or secondment are understood at the time the contract is agreed
- the extent to which these demands are relatively stable over the period of the placement
- the energy and commitment which the learner is prepared to invest in the contract – given the energy and commitment which their new job is likely to demand of them.

Learning contracts appear to work very well in these situations where the tutor has a good understanding of the placement or secondment, either from their own experience or by involving a third, knowledgeable party.

The ability of the learner to anticipate the demands and to commit to the contract is also important. For example, one learner completed his MBA programme on schedule by carrying out three learning contracts in the targeted time despite taking up a new and very responsible job in charge of a factory in Italy – at the same time relocating his family from England to Italy, and learning basic Italian. Other learners on the same programme, however, have sought permission to defer undertaking their contracts when faced with much smaller changes in work circumstances.

Three-way negotiations

Learning contracts may sometimes involve a third party, in addition to the learner and the tutor. In work-based learning contracts this may be the learner's line manager, or some other representative of the employer. In some cases it may be desirable to involve an additional specialist in the area where the learner wants to undertake a contract. There may indeed be three, four or even five people involved in the negotiation of a contract.

The advantages of involving a third party are usually to do with the additional information, expertise or authority they can contribute to the contract. A learner's line manager, for example, may provide easy access to information and resources it would be difficult to gain in any other way.

Where a third party is involved, they will need to be briefed about the principles of the programme, and the learning contract, and their role in it – preferably prior to the meeting where the contract is negotiated.

In Chapter 12 we shall consider a range of issues to do with the third party. Here we consider a specific point that can arise at the negotiation of the contract.

We previously stated that it is a fundamental principle of the learning contract approach that the learner should own the contract, because ownership of the learning contract gives rise to greater commitment to honouring it. Ownership comes about when the contract area has originated with the learner and they have set out, or participated in setting out, the objectives, the action plan and resources needed, and the performance measures.

It is sometimes evident in learning contract negotiations that the impetus for selecting a given area comes not from the learner but from their boss. The learner's boss may take control out of conviction that he/she knows best what the learner needs to develop, or because he/she feels more comfortable in a telling/directing role, or because there is a special, pet project he/she wants the learner to complete. It is often difficult in these situations to establish real ownership of the contract with the learner.

More explicitly than this, on a number of occasions I, and other tutors,

Box 7.6 The imposed contract

At the first of the three discussions to establish Vic's learning contracts for the CMS programme it was evident that there were differences of opinion between Vic and his boss. Alan, the Project Manager, found Vic disorganized, haphazard, badly prepared, and suggested Vic should do a time management contract.

Vic rejected this strenuously, and it was eventually agreed that his first learning contract would be in another area.

Throughout his period of involvement with the programme there were external difficulties – re-organization of his section, with enforced redundancies always a possibility, and wide fluctuations in the workload. It was also apparent that he was a poorly organized individual who overshot deadlines and failed to keep appointments. This realization was always resisted by Vic, who would point to all manner of reasons outside his control why he had not met his targets. Eventually he failed the programme: he ran out of time.

Generally an imposed contract requires the employer's representative to bring the problem to the learner's attention and gain agreement that it is a problem. If this is not done, the learning contract will not work as a means of correcting the problem. A more effective path will probably be disciplinary action for the performance failures.

have been asked by a manager to use a learning contract to help a more junior employee who 'has a problem'. Can learning contracts work under these circumstances? In my experience, such a learning contract will only be effective if the learner:

- accepts there is a problem
- believes something can be done about it
- is prepared to do something about it.

If any of these three conditions does not apply, learning is very unlikely to take place.

Three-way negotiations can result in much richer contracts than simple two-way agreements, but their dynamics can be more complex.

Review

The negotiation of each individual learning contract is a unique event, and the patient and receptive tutor, who helps each learner articulate and develop their self-determined proposals, can often learn as much as the

Box 7.7 Without moving your lips

The clearest sign of undue influence over the contract is when the line manager explains what the contract proposal is about.

The tutor might greet the learner and line manager, and after the initial pleasantries ask the learner, 'Have you decided what you want to do?'

'We think the contract should be about . . .' a voice replies, but it is not the learner's voice. This sometimes occurs with line managers who take a genuine, nurturing interest in developing their staff.

Where the direction has all taken place before the meeting, the learner might give the initial reply, with sideways glances to the line manager. If the learner has difficulty with the explanation the line manager will quickly come to the rescue and explain the proposal, suggesting it probably originated with him or her.

person they are helping. There are patterns to negotiations, however, common opportunities to enrich the contract process that should be seized, common problems that once recognized can be avoided.

In this chapter we have considered some common patterns that can affect work-based contracts and contracts which seek to develop the learners' skills.

Chapter 8

Agreeing assessment measures

In discussing learning contracts to this point, we have distinguished between *learning objectives* and *assessment measures*. Learning objectives specify what is to be learned, while assessment measures state what will be produced or demonstrated to prove that the learning objective has been achieved. In this sense the assessment measures act as more precise targets than the learning objectives themselves.

In fact, from agreeing the goal of the contract, to agreeing the learning objectives and then the assessment measures, the learner passes through a process of increasing specificity, funnelling and focusing the contract towards points that become more and more precise.

In Chapter 1 it was argued that assessment is an essential feature of an effective learning contract, and that the prospect of assessment considerably adds to the learner's focus and motivation. Of course, assessment is necessary if any kind of certification or recognition is to follow successful completion of the learning contract. However, a disadvantage of assessment may be that the original aim of the learning contract – personal learning and development – becomes subverted into the achievement of the assessment measures for the sake of the extrinsic reward. A cost of attaching a qualification to a learning contract is that the effort which could otherwise go solely towards self-development is divided between the linked goals of:

- learning and developing
- proving that learning and development have taken place.

Sometimes the division may be weighted towards the latter, unproductive goal at the expense of the former. A problem with the UK's National Vocational Qualifications (NVQs), particularly as they have been designed for higher-level jobs, has been that the processes of assessment have been seen as arduous and time-consuming, and also adding little value in terms of development of the individual's skills (Cheetham 1994).

In this chapter we consider some of the choices available to the learner

Box 8.1 From goal to assessment measures

The moves from the goal of the learning contract to the assessment measures should create a sharper focus and a funnelling of energy.

Goal	Learning objectives	Assessment measures
Example 1: Time management	Have a better understanding of how I am using my time and how this relates to the priorities of the job	A log of how I have spent my time on work or work-related matters for a two-week period, with each activity analysed as to priority, using the ABCX system of priorities. Oral explanation of this
Example 2: Assertiveness	Be more assertive in refusing unreasonable requests for assistance from managers in other departments	A written account of at least four occasions when I have refused unreasonable requests from other managers: an assessment of my behaviour as to how – honest, firm and direct – problem-centred – confident it was an assessment of my feelings as to whether I felt: – under pressure – guilty – angry – calm – confident.

and the tutor in terms of agreeing assessment measures that will be appropriate for a learning contract.

Measuring success

For each learning contract there are ideal methods of assessment, which accurately and efficiently evaluate the learning that has been undertaken. There are also, in most cases, limitations on the ideal. Some limitations are simply due to the uncooperative nature of reality, other constraints relate to the regulations of the particular learning programme (particularly if it leads to a qualification). The level of available resources (number of assessors, time available, equipment, etc.) will also limit what can be done. However, working within these limits it is possible to move closer towards an ideal form of assessment with the learning contract approach than with any other method of development. This is because the assessment measures are agreed as part of the contract, and so should be as snug a fit as the law, the budget and awkward reality will allow.

There are two obvious questions regarding the assessment of learning contracts: what evidence of learning is required? What standards must that evidence meet? The answers to both these questions should be set out as clearly as possible in the learning contract document.

Which takes us to a third question, less immediately obvious: who designs the assessment? Let us deal with this issue first.

Who designs the assessment?

The short answer to this question is: the assessment measures, like the rest of the learning contract, should be agreed by all the parties to the contract. In that sense the design of assessment measures is a joint venture.

This is true, so far as it goes. But while the tutor is advised to stay well clear of proposing new learning objectives it may be appropriate for the tutor to take more initiatives here, including proposing new measures of assessment. There are five good reasons why this should be so.

1. The success of the learning contract will depend on the achievement of targets proposed in assessment, so these must be more precise than any other part of the learning contract. The need to change the learner's original proposal is more likely to arise in this section of the contract than any other. This occurs, in part, for the following reason.

2. Learners seem to have more difficulty preparing assessment measures than designing any other area of the learning contract. They will often put forward inappropriate or vague suggestions. This may be because they don't know the detail of the area they are about to study, or simply because they lack experience in linking learning to assessment. The tutor should have a better understanding of the subject area, and will have a better grasp of the principles of learning and assessment than most learners in this position, and will be able to make suggestions that are recognized as logical and reasonable.

3. There may be particular regulations governing assessment if the contract is part of a programme leading to a qualification. The tutor is likely to be more familiar with these regulations than the learner, and so the learner is likely to defer to the tutor's expertise at this point.

4. The sense of ownership, which is important to the success of the learning contract method, should already have been established if the learner has chosen the learning area and has proposed learning objectives and

---

Box 8.2 The blank box

The learner who is exploring an area such as information technology for the first time is ill-equipped to suggest assessment measures for a learning contract, and this is a clear case of the initiative naturally coming from the tutor. Assessment measures for a learning contract that sees a learner taking the first steps in using a database might be as follows.

1. Production of a database constructed on a standard package: to contain data relevant to my job, and to contain at least 20 files and eight fields. Access to the data will be through at least three fields.
2. Demonstration of ability to use the database by accessing the data, adding a new file, correcting detail in a file.
3. Oral explanation of how database programs could be used in other areas of my job (if applicable).
4. Oral report on any barriers, problems or difficulties I encountered in tackling the contract, and how I overcame them.

This last point is to encourage the learner to reflect explicitly upon his or her experiences, with an emphasis on successful achievement. It may help the learner to make realistic plans for further developments in understanding and using computers and/or in designing any future learning contracts.

---

a plan of action which have been accepted with no more than minor amendments. Proposals to change the assessment measures, if they are reasonably discussed and agreed, should not seriously threaten that proprietorial feeling.

5. Where a number of learners are undertaking learning contracts as part of a programme, the tutor who is involved in several contracts may legitimately suggest a raising or lowering of standards – involving additions or subtractions in the assessment area – to ensure parity between participants.

Of course, like the rest of the learning contract, the assessment measures should be agreed by all the parties to the contract, and not imposed by the tutor. It is also good practice for the tutor to ask for proposals from the learner, rather than to assume that this is an area where the learner will look to the tutor for ideas and suggestions.

The tutor's role here is ideally to clarify the vague points of the learner's proposal, perhaps to suggest that some proposed assessment measures are unnecessary, to put forward replacements or additions, and to be able to explain the reasons for each of these actions.

Who assesses the contract?

The rules regarding who will assess the contract will be strongly influenced by the regulations governing the programme.

On one non-qualification programme, for example, the learner is under an obligation to report back to a group of colleagues and the tutor, but it is the learner's judgement whether or not the contract has been completed.

On another programme, the agreement is that the contract is assessed by the parties who agree it in the first place – the learner, the tutor and the learner's line manager. A veto system applies, so that each of these three must judge the contract to be complete.

On the Master's programme first described at Box 2.1, the written evidence is assessed by the tutor who negotiated the contract, a second marker from the programme team, and an external examiner; the accompanying oral presentation is assessed by at least three members of the examination board.

What kind of evidence?

In designing the assessment of learning contracts on academic programmes, where the main dynamic of the contract will be to research a particular area of knowledge or activity, the main form of assessment is normally a written report, or dissertation, perhaps accompanied by an oral presentation and questions. The length of the report should be agreed, and its style (perhaps by reference to other reports which the learner can look at) and the main areas of content – the chapter headings and a summary of the issues that will be addressed: these may be expressed in terms of ideas and/or writers and sources that the learner must show they understand.

Where the contract aims to develop a particular skill the possible range of evidence appears more diverse. Work on higher-level NVQs/SVQs has wrestled with a very similar issue of how a person can prove competence at a particular level of performance (Eraut 1994, Chapter 9; Eraut and Cole 1993; Mitchell 1993; Wolf 1994). With simple skills, the easiest way might be to arrange a demonstration. Sit me before a computer terminal and I will use a spreadsheet, add to it, draw from it, amend its shape. Similarly, with analytical skills, a demonstration is relatively simple to arrange: bring me a balance sheet and I will demonstrate my ability to read and analyse it. And so on.

But many practical skills are not amenable to demonstration on demand. Skills such as conducting disciplinary interviews, for example, are only demonstrated behind closed doors. Skills such as time management or team leading may be seen only in hundreds of small actions over reasonably long

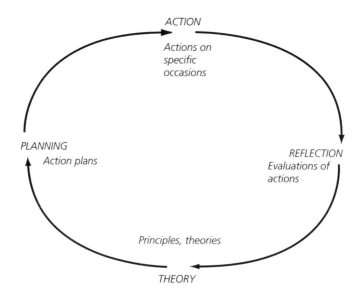

Figure 8.1   The Learning Cycle

periods of time. These are the problems of assessment facing higher-level NVQs/SVQs.

To solve the problems, we might in some cases set up a simulation, where I (the learner) can demonstrate the skill. In other cases you (the tutor) might have to believe my account of what I have done. Perhaps the testimony of witnesses to my performance would help to convince you. Perhaps the results of my skilled behaviour, measured in cost or productivity terms. In the UK, higher-level NVQs/SVQs have taken an approach of using a portfolio of different types of evidence.

In picking a path through the options of types of evidence, it is good to bear in mind the relevant principles of skill development. You will remember from Chapter 2 that a learner develops a skill by going through a series of stages, set out as points on the Learning Cycle (Figure 8.1). The structure of the Learning Cycle can be used to design the components of the assessment.

Action is the demonstration of skilled behaviour. This may be demonstrable on demand; or there may be records of it; or – at the very least – the learner can describe it.

Reflection is the learner's evaluation of behaviour: strictly speaking it is a reflection on their own behaviour, but this can in practice be extended to include evaluation of the behaviour of others. The learner's reflections can place examples of skilled behaviour in a broader context.

Theory is the understanding of principles and frameworks, ranging from the grasp of complex models to the use of rules of thumb. A good understanding of the theoretical frameworks that underpin skilled performance may derive from published material on the subject mediated by the learner's own experiences.

Planning is the process of looking ahead to consider the next opportunities for both action and development.

To assess the development of a skill, it may be appropriate to assess evidence from various points on the Learning Cycle.

Action: can the learner provide sample demonstrations of the skill? Or convincing evidence that such demonstrations have taken place?

Reflection: can they evaluate these sample demonstrations and explain, say, how it might be appropriate to behave differently in other circumstances? Can they explain how these demonstrations represent an improvement on previous levels of performance?

Theory: can the learner explain some of the principles, or the ideas, or the key points, it is important to follow in using this skill?

Planning: can the learner identify what further development of the skill they propose to undertake? Can they explain how they intend to use this skill in the future?

Considering some evidence from the different points of the Learning Cycle will often improve the assessment of even a very observable skill, such as the ability to make presentations. The extent to which each point needs to be sampled will depend in part on the skill area and in part on the regulations governing the programme. With less easily demonstrable skills, the tutor may wish to see more substantial evidence from reflection, theory and planning.

The evidence that we have seen from the four points of the Learning Cycle may all originate with the learner. This may make some readers feel uncomfortable. How do we know, you may ask, that the evidence is genuine?

On programmes of pure self-development this is rarely a key issue. Learners will often reflect quite honestly on this matter, and sometime will even express concern about whether they *really* have developed, and devise better and better ways of evaluating their learning. On programmes linked to qualifications, however, the learners' motives may be mixed. Whether or not they have actually developed their target skill, they have a certain interest in claiming that they have done so, in order to gain the qualification. This can lead to a certain amount of self-deception, some inflated claims for development, and occasional (but rare) outright dishonesty.

The criteria we can use to evaluate evidence of skill development are:

- authenticity: the evidence should be genuine

- validity: the evidence should relate to the skills that are the target of the contract
- reliability: the evidence should be representative of the learner's capability.

We will return to these points in more detail in Chapter 11, when we look at the process of assessment.

With this in mind, let us consider the different forms of evidence we might use to assess skill development.

Forms of evidence

Depending on the programme and its aims and regulations, the available resources, the learner's situation and the specific contract area, we might consider a number of different forms of evidence.

- *A report from the learner* – either written or oral, which may include any or all of the points above on Action, Reflection, Theory and Planning.
- *Demonstration of the skill* – either in a natural or in a simulated setting; this may be observed directly by the assessor, or a recording of some kind may be made available.
- *Testimony from other people* who have observed the learner carrying out the skilled performance.
- *Products or outcomes* which are the result of the learner's behaviour, or which corroborate claims made through other forms of evidence.

Let us look at each of these in turn. This may be familiar ground to those readers with experience of higher-level NVQ or SVQ programmes, who may wish to jump ahead to the following section on establishing assessment criteria for a contract.

A report from the learner

We have argued that it is beneficial to sample evidence from all four points of the Learning Cycle. The only way that this can be done is by gathering information from the learners themselves. This may be in writing, or in the form of an oral presentation, or in an interview – or in all three forms.

The programme regulations are likely to influence the form – with an inclination towards a written report for qualification programmes. If an oral presentation or a *viva voce* is a serious, separately evaluated part of the assessment, some regulations call for it to be recorded on video-tape or audio-tape. Obviously, the length and shape of any written report will be affected by programme regulations, and may range from a 20 000-word piece of work to a short list of key principles the learner has found useful in developing a skill.

Whatever the specific form, at the end of the contract the learner may be expected to:

- give an account of what he or she did in pursuit of the contract objectives and what happened as a result of these actions
- summarize what he or she has learned as a result of this
- set out a plan for future action.

The requirement to produce specific points in writing can concentrate the mind (e.g. 'a clear and realistic action plan to make further improvements in skill over the next six months', 'a list of the skills I feel are important in interviewing, together with a rating of where I stand in each category'). On the other hand, the requirement to produce a written report can divert significant amounts of effort from the development of the skill itself, and may place too much emphasis (and reward) on the skills of report writing to the exclusion of others.

The oral report, on the other hand, enables a to and fro between assessor and learner, saves the learner time, and concentrates on what was done and what was learned rather than what has been written about it. The assessor is able to seek the level of detail he/she requires about what the learner did and said.

In general, the written form is appropriate for summary (what have I learned? where do I still need to develop?) and for outline (a list of the actions I undertook); the oral form is appropriate for the detailed accounts of what I did, the reasons why I feel I have learned the target skills, my rationale for my learning strategy.

The Behavioural Event interview approach (Chapter 5) of seeking a very detailed account of actions, thoughts and feelings can form the basis of the oral report. A *learning log* of events and reflections on them can provide a written equivalent.

Demonstration

The learner demonstrates to the assessor that he or she can perform the actions that make up the skill. This may usefully be accompanied by some discussion and explanation.

As we have said, demonstration is particularly appropriate for contracts where it is easy to replicate the skill. Demonstration is generally not practical in the interpersonal skill areas – although there may be some exceptions, such as presentation skills – or in situations where the occasion on which the skill will be displayed is so unpredictable, or where exercise of the skill takes place over a long period of time.

Where natural performance of the skill is not practical it is tempting to explore simulation – a set of circumstances that should test the skills. If it is not possible for the assessor to observe, say, an actual recruitment interview, why not set up a mock interview, which can be observed and assessed?

Simulation, however, is subject to problems of transferability: is the simulation a valid and reliable test of the target skill, so that the assessment of performance in the simulation can be taken for the presence of skill in a real situation? Much depends on the extent to which the simulation either resembles actual circumstances in which the learner will use the skills to be assessed, or the extent to which it is a fair test of generic skills the learner has undertaken to develop.

Audio and video recordings are frequent companions to simulations, particularly for set pieces such as interviews, presentations or meetings. Video does provide an enduring record of the performance, of course, and can enable a learner to comment critically on his/her performance after the event – this commentary may be included as part of the assessment. What is said and omitted in the commentary often gives a better indication of the learner's awareness of the skill than the contents of the tape itself. There are certain potential drawbacks.

- Video equipment may lend a further air of unreality to a simulation, although improvements in the technology in recent years have led to cameras becoming more discreet.
- Video distorts some aspects of behaviour, making hesitations, ums and ahs and some aspects of body language appear much more significant than they are in reality. The danger of assessing what is on the video-tape because it is easy to assess should be guarded against if the aim of the learning contract is to improve the exercise of a skill in the workplace.
- Viewing and assessing a video-tape (as in directly viewing a demonstration) is often time-consuming for the assessor.

Audio taping is less obtrusive than video recording and may be of value in capturing a record of real action, where video would be impossible but the assent of other parties may be given to taping the meeting, or the interview. This will never be more than a partial record of action, of course, but it can provide a piece of evidence on which questions and further explanations can be based. Again, it is time-consuming to assess.

Testimony

The testimony of others can be a helpful element in assessment of a contract.

- The other person will be a natural witness to the exercise of the skill that is targeted by the learning contract, and where it would be impossible or inconvenient for the assessor to be present.
- The other person is an expert witness, by virtue of his/her special

Box 8.3 The expert witness

When learners use the detail of their real work environment as part of their learning contract, it can create a difficulty for the tutor. The planning report looks well structured, but its contents are beyond the tutor's technical knowledge: the learner sets out the priorities he believes the department should apply – and the tutor has little idea of whether or not these are realistic: another learner brings along the proof that she can use Force Field Analysis – a report on the factors that influenced a particular committee on a recent decision – and the tutor needs someone who can verify the facts.

In these cases the tutor can test the logical consistency of the learner's viewpoint, and by raising questions of detail may be able to assess some dimensions of credibility or depth of understanding, but it is necessary to be able to turn to someone who has real knowledge (usually the learner's boss) or expert knowledge (the company finance manager, export manager, systems analyst, etc.) and ask for confirmation of the accuracy of the facts. Learners will almost always accept and respect this.

knowledge: the most frequent occurrence of this is likely to be when this is local knowledge of the learner's organization, its procedures and priorities, but it may also be specialist professional knowledge – of, say, accounting or project management or operational techniques.

It is often worth checking the availability of witnesses with the learner, and discussing what kind of testimony they might provide, and how they can be approached. If the witness is to provide an opinion about whether something was of a sufficient standard, accurate enough, authentic, adhering to company policy – in other words anything more than attesting to factual occurrences – he/she must be briefed as to the role to be played and criteria to be used. It may be helpful to specify in the contract the aspects of performance that a witness will evaluate, or even to discuss the design of structured questionnaires to obtain evaluative feedback.

Products and outcomes

Some skills result in the creation of products: the exercise of manual/artistic skills such as carpentry and pottery have obvious tangible results. Report-writing skills, and certain analytical skills, produce paper 'products' which can be shown to an assessor and evaluated.

Product evidence has become very popular with the increasing use of NVQ assessment measures, where some of the 'products' are not the result

---

Box 8.4 Assessing outcomes

Phil developed a learning contract that was linked to a complex organizational change project. He was a senior manager in a large retail organization, and the company was being reorganized to decentralize certain functions. This meant that much more responsibility would be passed down to the managers of individual stores, who reported to Phil, and they would be expected to take more initiatives. It was Phil's responsibility to help the store managers to take on their new role. This was the organizational change project.

Phil's learning objectives concerned changing his own style of leadership from a strong preference for command and control to an ability to facilitate and empower. This would be central to the success of the change project.

One of the outcomes, which was reviewed at the end of the contract, was the reaction and performance of the store managers: in other words, Phil's success in the change project. But other measures were more important in assessing Phil's success in changing his leadership style.

---

of the learner's actions, but simply pieces of corroborative evidence or published background information – such as minutes of meetings, organization charts, etc. Their value must be weighed carefully against the effort it takes the learner to collect and file them, and the assessor to read and evaluate them.

Learners may invite assessment of a contract by its outcomes.

The junior manager who wishes to learn how to improve his team's morale might offer an improvement in productivity as the best measure, and in a similar vein the learner who wishes to develop her marketing skills might suggest increased sales as the most appropriate yardstick. Training skills? Will the trainees learn more quickly? Negotiating skills? Will the other side accept my proposals?

There is a danger, in each of these areas, that the behaviour of others, apart from the learner, is being assessed. The assessment might penalize bad luck or reward good luck and in either case overlook the degree of skill that has been developed.

Assessment criteria

Having defined the form and some of the content of the evidence that the learner will produce, the parties to the contract need to address the question: what standards must this evidence meet?

Box 8.5 A good presentation

Jennifer's learning contract on improving her presentation skills included the following terms.
  The presentation will be assessed on the extent to which:

1. It achieves or can be shown to have pursued its objectives (the objectives are to be stated to the tutor before the presentation).
2. It is well structured.
3. It keeps the attention of the average member of the audience.
4. Delivery is clear and confident.
5. Visual aids are clear and appropriate.

And there are no significant weaknesses in any of these five areas.

Indications of the standards may be set out in the contract: for example, an academic research report must show a good understanding of the key facts and ideas in the area of study; it must show an ability to apply theories and frameworks to events; it must be able to do this clearly, concisely, accurately, reasonably, logically. These are examples of the type of criteria that may be applied. It is clear, however, that there still remains a need for judgement – someone needs to say whether the learner's report represents a 'good understanding', whether it has included a sufficient number of the 'key facts and ideas in the area of study' and whether it has done so sufficiently 'clearly, concisely, accurately', etc. In many academic programmes this judgement of the appropriate standard of a piece of work rests with tutors, who make their evaluation on the basis of experience with other programmes of the same academic level. This may be acknowledged explicitly within the learning contract: e.g. 'the report will be of a level appropriate to the final stage of a Master's degree' or 'the report will be evaluated by Professor Jones' (Knowles 1986, pp 68–69, 132–139).

On a skills development contract the forms of evidence and the criteria may be more varied. For example, the learner might propose to demonstrate his or her increased skill in making formal presentations by giving a presentation on a particular topic, and including the assessor in the audience.

First, to clarify what might be expected, it would be good practice for the tutor to establish agreement on the size of the audience and the length of the presentation. Secondly, some criteria concerning the quality of the presentation, or a means of establishing these criteria, should be agreed. Thus, learner and tutor might agree:

- a set of criteria that are discussed and written in an agreed format when the learning contract is drawn up

- to use a pre-established set of criteria for the skill area from some published source
- that the learner will research the area and propose a set of criteria by which the presentation might be judged. These must be realistic in terms of what is generally regarded as competent performance, and must be agreed before the presentation is given.

Thirdly, some means of establishing what learning or development has taken place should be agreed. The likely form of this will be a type of personal report, comparing previous performance with that demonstrated at the end of the learning contract. It is advisable to define some aspects of this report: will it be written or oral? Must it find some improvement has taken place? Roughly what length should the report be? Perhaps we could also agree that the report should be credible and convincing, and seek to provide evidence of improvement where possible, rather than relying entirely on assertion.

Review

It may be clear now that the aims of the tutor to ensure that an learning contract is realistic, precise and clear are nowhere more important than in the area of assessment. A clear picture of the type, content and nature of the evidence that will be produced must be established, together with explicit agreement on the measures against which it will be assessed.

As a tutor, you have more scope for intervention here than elsewhere in the learning contract, for taking the initiative in making proposals and for suggesting alternatives to the ideas put forward by the learner. But to make full use of the potential of the learning contract approach, tutors must remember that they do not have a free hand. Assessment measures must be agreed with the learner, not imposed without consent, and tutors must be careful not to change the learning contract out of all recognition by including radical new items at the assessment stage.

Chapter 9

Negotiation skills

Sometimes learning contracts are agreed quickly and easily: the learner presents a clear and acceptable proposal which requires minimal addition or alteration and little support, and after a few questions and a short conversation the contract can be signed. At other times the negotiation is very difficult, and both parties struggle to reach a clear agreement. Some common problems have been identified in the previous three chapters.

In talking about the ease or difficulty of making a contract, of course, we are reflecting on the process of reaching agreement. A contract can also be judged after the event – how successful was it in helping the person to learn and develop? There is no necessary correlation between the ease or difficulty of agreeing a contract, and the degree of learning and development that ensues.

In this chapter we take a final look at the business of agreeing the contract, and consider the skills that are needed by a tutor who wants to be an effective negotiator. The skills are not unique to negotiating learning contracts: we can see similarities with the skills of negotiating in other circumstances, with the abilities needed to be an effective coach and facilitator – and with general good communication practice.

Negotiation models

There are a number of models of negotiation, and of negotiating skills. They have been developed from commercial and sales negotiations, and industrial relations scenarios.

Conflicting aims

In many negotiating situations there is an implication that, while the objectives of the parties may overlap, there are potential conflicts of interest

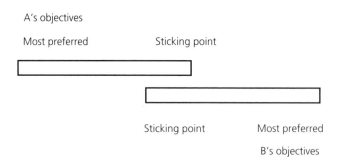

Figure 9.1   Overlapping objectives based on Kennedy (1984 *et al.*)

which are resolved through trade-offs and compromises. In negotiating learning contracts – as in other negotiations – much depends on the circumstances. Where the contracts are part of a programme leading to a qualification, the aims and roles of the parties are potentially more complex than where contracts are simply being used for personal development.

- The learner is concerned not only with personal learning and development but also with being able to demonstrate achievement in order to attain the qualification. Learners may seek to minimize the risk involved in undertaking the contract under these circumstances.
- The tutor is concerned not only with what the learner wants to do, but also with the regulations of the programme, governing the area of the contract, and its size or challenge.

The model of overlapping objectives can be a useful visual image in some negotiations: the tutor seeking more challenge, or a greater size of contract in some respects, the learner seeking something more easily achievable (Figure 9.1).

Stages of negotiation

There are also a number of stage models of negotiation, which aim to set out common sequences of events or phases of discussion (Kennedy *et al.* 1984).

The negotiation of a learning contract is a fluid affair, where effective explorations of objectives, action plans and assessment measures may take place in no systematic order. However, a simple model of the various stages might be represented as below.

1. Welcome and establish rapport.
2. Receive and discuss the learner's proposal, especially:

   a) main points – clarify any ambiguities

b) reasons for tackling this area
c) contingencies – check for dependencies in the action plan
d) resource needs – check for dependencies, check on requirements and availability
e) assessment measures – clarify and amend, or develop, as needed.

3. Sign and confirm agreement, and/or arrange next steps – such as a revised proposal, an interim meeting, or resources that the tutor will provide, or a meeting to assess the contract.

This assumes that the learner will present a proposal. An alternative model might be as follows.

1. Welcome and establish rapport.
2. Discussion of learner's broad ideas – which may be based around needs and/or opportunities.
3a. Establish the goal, then learning objectives, action plan, resources, assessment points; or
3b. Establish an outline action plan (based on opportunities), then learning objectives, goal, resources, assessment points.
4. Sign and confirm agreement, and/or arrange next steps – such as a revised proposal, an interim meeting, or resources that the tutor will provide, or a meeting to assess the contract.

Both of these models are broad approximations to the reality of effective negotiation. For example, rapport – neatly addressed at point 1 in both models – may need to be re-established at various points throughout the discussion. The main points – or the learner's priorities – may require further confirmation as the proposal is developed: will this detailed proposal actually meet the reasons the learner described for choosing a contract in this area? The general trend of both models holds true, but the line between the different stages is more blurred and more often breached than the neat list would indicate.

Unfreezing and freezing

A useful model which can apply to processes that take place during the contract is the model of unfreezing/shaping/freezing, first developed by Kurt Lewin to describe the process of changing a person's attitudes. In the context of learning contracts, the model is often less about persuasion and more about helping the learner to think creatively.

The first stage is of *unfreezing* – getting the person to relax or question a fixed perception. In the learning contract process, this might begin during the priming and needs analysis stages, where a learner may come to identify new development needs, and believe that they can improve on current levels of knowledge or skill. During the contract negotiation more unfreezing may

---

Box 9.1 The effective negotiator

Negotiators of learning contracts can benefit from some research into negotiations in other spheres. Neil Rackham and John Carlisle made a study of the differences in the behaviours between 'skilled' and 'average' negotiators in industrial relations and commercial matters.

It is relevant to learning contracts that skilled negotiators appear to spend more time on:

- seeking information
- summaries
- test of mutual understanding
- commentaries on their own feelings

than 'average' negotiators.
Rackham and Carlisle 1978

---

take place, in particular as the learner re-evaluates their proposed contract area and their action plan.

The second stage is of *shaping*: in a classic situation of persuasion or influence, one person attempts to shape the other person's ideas. A tutor will often try to influence or persuade during the contract negotiation – making suggestions about extending the contract here, reducing it there, re-shaping it in some other place – but in many cases the efforts of the tutor will go into drawing a shape for the agreement from the learner, and encouraging the learner to feel a high level of commitment to the contract.

The third stage is of *freezing* (or re-freezing): gaining confirmation from the learner of their commitment to the contract. This is achieved partly through the written document – which may be formally signed as a symbol of this commitment – and partly through checking, at various stages of the discussion, the learner's level of acceptance of the contract.

This useful model comes to life in those negotiations when the learner re-evaluates their original proposal, perhaps seeks some reassurance or confirmation from the tutor, and produces a better, more satisfying, more effective contract.

The skills of the tutor

The key skills of the tutor at the negotiation stage of the contract might be summarized as:

- reminding the learner of principles and parameters

- gathering information
- provoking reflection
- making suggestions and recommendations
- providing encouragement
- summarizing and checking understanding.

All of these are underpinned by a realistic evaluation of the contract proposal.

Principles and parameters

Part of the role of the tutor is to set out the principles and parameters of the contract: for example, reminding the learner (and any other parties to the contract) of the basic principles of the process, such as the operation of the Learning Cycle, the importance of identifying realistic targets for staged improvement, and the fact that ownership of the contract should lie with the learner. These are all principles of contract learning that we have previously encountered. Part of the tutor's role is also to remind the learner of the parameters of the contract, and to police them.

The learning contract approach provides great flexibility within a supporting structure. It is part of the tutor's role to remind others of the shape of the structure, and the limits of flexibility, and this at times requires clear statements with no promise of movement or compromise. Typical statements of this type are:

'The contract needs to acknowledge the published body of knowledge in this area.'

'The learning contract must be about some aspect of managing – not to do with the technical side of your job.'

'This proposal is a project, not a learning contract. In using learning contracts we are concerned with what you are going to learn, not what you are going to do.'

'We must agree the contract before you set about doing it. You can't write up the targets after you have achieved them: that's not acceptable.'

The first example in this list – about understanding the main published ideas in the contract area – may lead the tutor to give advice about texts and writers who must be acknowledged. Care must be taken here. It is sometimes necessary for tutors new to the learning contract approach to spend time identifying for themselves the boundaries of the areas where they can make directive statements and still remain effective negotiators.

Some programmes have more complex parameters than others. This can create an unfortunate dynamic of tutor direction at the contract negotiation. Effective work on priming the learner can minimize this effect.

Gathering information and provoking reflection

The two skills areas of gathering information and provoking reflection merge with one another. They are based on effective listening and on thoughtful questions.

Negotiators need to listen and to encourage the learner to speak. Therefore, they will use more questions than any other type of statement. Some questions are used to gain more information about the proposal, the reasons for the proposal and the existing level of skill or knowledge of the learner.

In particular, it is good practice as a tutor to make sure you have an accurate understanding of the proposal itself. Simple questions are necessary, based on the written proposal. For example:

'What do you mean by "interview people"?'
'What do you mean by "interviewing skills"?'
'How long will this take?'
'How many people will you interview?'
'Where will you do the work?'

These questions can serve two important purposes:

- They enable you, as the tutor, to establish a clear picture of the learning contract in your own mind, such that you can think more easily about its realism, about what support may be needed, and about what assessment is appropriate.
- They may enable formation of a clearer picture in the mind of the learner about what he or she is going to do. They also emphasize the learner's ownership of, and responsibility for, the learning contract. Interspersed with suggestions from the tutor, they will lead to a more precise and realistic contract – and one which has a greater motivational effect on the learner who undertakes it.

Estimating the degree of difficulty of the learning contract and setting this within a realistic time frame is a fundamental part of the tutor's role. To estimate the realism of a target the tutor must consider, as well as the learner's entry behaviour, the proposed action plan:

- the various activities, including reflection and evaluation, that make up the plan
- the amount of time it will take to undertake each one
- the scheduling of any learning opportunities included in the learning contract
- the desired or proposed schedule of the contract
- the amount of time available to the learner to undertake the action plan.

Box 9.2 Exploring a proposal: questioning and suggesting

James presented his first learning contract proposal in a direct and clear manner: he wanted to improve his skills in assessing people who worked for him. To this end, he proposed to set up an appraisal system and to operate it for the eight weeks of the contract, and then report on the skills he had developed.

James had a responsible job as the manager of a day-care centre for a local authority. His line manager was not interested in the management development programme, and was not involved in discussing the contract.

Was there an appraisal scheme in the centre at present? asked the tutor.

No, there was not.

How many people worked in the centre?

About thirty-five.

And how many of them would the scheme cover?

Oh, all of them.

Were they all doing the same kind of jobs?

No. There was a wide variety of jobs. The staff were spread across seven or eight different grades, because of an historical anomaly. This contract might sort that out, too.

Was there a trade union?

Most of the staff belonged to a trade union that, at that time, opposed appraisal schemes.

Were there clear job descriptions to work from?

No. That would all need doing.

At this point the tutor voiced the opinion that this was a very large contract indeed, and perhaps the way forward was to break it into manageable pieces. What would be the first step? It would be to establish clear job specifications. Had James done that before? James had not. He began a learning contract on job analysis. By the time he reached the end he realized that his original vision of operating an appraisal system was a twelve-month project, not an eight-week contract.

By questioning in these areas, the tutor can help the learner to set realistic targets within a given time.

Other questions will call for more reflection from the learner. For example:

'What do you really want to do in this contract?'
'What are you going to learn?'
'Which of these two options will be most effective?'

Occasionally, with indecisive or ill-prepared learners, the tutor must be ready to endure long silences following these questions. The other main difficulty, for tutors who are comfortable with a more directive style, is that of suppressing their own preferences and assessments at this stage.

Of course, having asked the question, it is important to listen carefully to the answer. Some tutors, new to learning contracts, evidently engage in such great mental struggles to slot what the learner is saying into a convenient category of their own devising that they miss much of what they are being told.

Part of the tutor's job is to make some exploration of the learner's initial level of competence, in order to gauge the realism and the stretch of the contract. Good questions include:

'What is new about this?'
'Haven't you done this before?'
'What do you know about (this area) now?'
'What do you expect to learn?'
'What will you be able to do at the end of this contract that you can't do now?'
'What aspect of that skill will you increase during this contract?'
'How will you know you have improved that skill?'
'Is there any way you could prove that you can do that better?'

And when designing the action plan, a questioning approach to dependencies can be helpful:

'What if the meetings are cancelled?'
'What will you do if you can't get a copy of the book?'
'What if the training course doesn't run?'
'Are there other people you could interview?'

This non-directional guidance makes the learner consider contingency plans. The process of considering the possibility that this may not work out precisely according to the original simple plan is a beneficial one. Discussing even basic contingency plans is one step nearer towards putting them into action, if the need arises.

Exploration of the reasons for a contract proposal and the reasons for any of the proposed activities which may not be immediately obvious is a valuable exercise. This is to guard against the problems that arise when a learner jumps to conclusions – for example, concerning the skills he/she needs to develop in order to solve a problem, or about the connections between two different areas of study. Too many questions, or too firm a challenge, in this area can affect a learner's motivation and confidence, however, and it is wise to proceed with caution.

Box 9.3 Questioning and challenging

Probing and querying the reasons why a learner has picked a particular skill area is a recipe for a long discussion which may not produce a choice any better than the initial proposal.

All manner of doubts can surround the beginning of the learning contract.

For example, as a learner I may decide to improve my ability to make a good first impression: to appear positive, in control and organized.

There may be some doubts in my mind as to:

- whether I can do this. Aren't positive, self-confident people born, not made?
- whether I can trust you, the tutor, with the disclosure that I wish I could be more self-confident, positive, etc.
- whether other areas of development might not really be of a higher priority (but I can only choose one!).

To some extent the fear of the challenge, the fear of disclosure, the fear of making the wrong choice, can affect every contract proposal and unless there are very good reasons why a learner should not go ahead with the original suggestion it is probably best not to question it too closely. Learners can learn a great deal by tackling a contract in slightly the wrong area, and being brought face to face with this. As long as they have been responsible for choosing the contract, they may reflect upon their own choices and self-evaluations.

Suggestions and recommendations

The tutor may also make suggestions and recommendations about aspects of the learning contract. Of course, these might be phrased as guiding questions:

'Have you thought about practising this in team meetings?'
'Would it be possible to involve other members of the team in giving feedback?'
'Is there anyone who could evaluate the marketing plan you'll put forward?'
'Is it possible to produce copies of the agendas of the meetings?'
'Would that be enough to show you have reached that objective?'
'Would there be time to fit in another interview?'

or as suggestions:

'Perhaps you could practise this in team meetings.'

'You need to practise this in some way. Perhaps you could use the team meetings.'
'If you could involve other members of the team, and get their feedback, it would be helpful.'

One of the roles of the tutor here may be to recommend books, video-tapes or other sources of information which may help the learner, or to recommend techniques he/she could try.

Tutors new to negotiating learning contracts should be careful not to slip too gratefully into the familiar role of lecturer/expert/font of wisdom at this point, under the guise of providing legitimate advice about resources. A way of monitoring your own behaviour, to guard against exercising undue influence, is to check the words you use in making the recommendation:

'You could read/do/try this.'
'This might be helpful.'

leave more scope for choice than the loaded

'You should read/do/try this.'
'You must . . .'
'You ought to . . .'

This is not to legislate against vehemence or firm recommendations. At times they may be necessary. But if a concern of the tutor is for the learner to exercise choice and ownership over the contract, it is wise to avoid the parental imperatives of 'should', 'must' and 'ought' as much as possible.

Summarize and check understanding

A summary of the position, or of the options open to a learner, can be helpful in progressing the negotiation. Simply re-stating what the learner has said can clarify the basis of the contract: for example:

'So you want to set out a survey of attitudes to show the effects of the change?'

A typical response to a large and vague contract proposal may be:

'I can see two learning areas here: the investigation of the change process, and the study of how the policy is made. Which is most important to you?'

'It seems to me there are two areas here: the training and the marketing. From what you've said, either one of them could make a contract on its own. I think we need to decide which one we're going to go for.'

Summaries are simply good communications practice.

At times it may be helpful to check with simple statements about what appears to be happening:

Box 9.4 Questions and statements

It is possible to convey roughly the same meaning in questions and statements, but some of the nuances are important in the learning contract agreement.

'Is it necessary to do this?'

can be translated as

'I don't think it's necessary to do this.'

which can be translated as

'It's not necessary to do this.'

From the first question to the final, flat statement, we are doing two things:

- reducing the likelihood of the learner volunteering information
- reducing the ownership and control the learner may feel for the learning contract.

In the same way we could render:

'Will you be able to do all this in the time available?'

as

'I don't think you'll be able to do all this.'

and

'Would there be time to fit in another interview?'

as

'You need to carry out at least one more interview.'

with similar results.

'You don't look too sure.'
'This seems important to you.'

The final summary of the contract will be in writing, on the contract form.

Who should make this summary? The tutor? The learner? In the light of what we have said so far about ownership, it should be the learner – but they may need help, particularly in the first contract they undertake.

In the case of short contracts, where the aim is to discuss and draft the contract agreement in one meeting, the tutor may usefully produce a draft

---

Box 9.5 Another view of skills

We have seen that there are similarities between some aspects of action learning and the use of learning contracts. The characteristics of an action learning set adviser have been described as:

1. An ability to tolerate ambiguity – resulting in part from allowing the learners to take control of the process.
2. A quality of openness and frankness, which includes an ability to express one's own feelings in the learning situation.
3. A great deal of patience.
4. A desire to help people to learn and a belief in this method of learning.
5. Being able to put oneself into the other person's shoes and empathize with them.

These characteristics all appear extremely relevant to the negotiation of effective learning contracts.
Casey 1993

---

on the spot, with much questioning of the learner, using the learner's words wherever possible, and checking for acceptability of the final draft.

With longer contracts, where there may be less immediate time pressure to reach agreement, there is more of a case for leaving the drafting of this final summary with the learner.

If a draft contract is discussed and perhaps amended at a meeting, it is good practice to make sure both parties leave the meeting with a copy of the draft. This creates a record for both tutor and learner of the summary of the agreement to date.

Encouragement and support

Learners can be apprehensive about tackling a contract area. They may be so at the outset – unsure about whether to broach the topic of a possible contract area – and at the end, when they review the draft of their action plan and assessment targets. Encouragement at this stage is valuable. Simply reassuring a learner that you believe they can be successful in a particular contract area can help to allay many of their doubts.

When a learning contract has been agreed, encouraging statements such as:

'This looks like a good contract.'
'I'm looking forward to seeing the results of this.'

Box 9.6 Coaching skills

The list of skills needed by an effective coach, produced by Kalinauckas and King, appears relevant to tutors who are using learning contracts. It includes the skills of:

active listening
questioning
giving praise and recognition
building rapport
being non-judgmental
being candid and challenging
being able to work from other people's agendas
giving encouragement and support
getting to the point.

Kalinauckas and King 1994

can help to motivate the learner and confirm their choices.

Displays of understanding, agreement and empathy can also help:

'I know it can be difficult to do this.'
'I can see why you want to do something about it.'
'I understand the problem.'

During the learner's explanation of the proposal, non-verbal confirmations – the nod of the head, the regular eye contact, the 'uh-huh' sounds that say 'I am listening' – help to support and encourage. The absence of any such confirmation, combined with the questions which are a necessary part of the tutor's role, can create an atmosphere some learners find inhibiting and intimidating.

The corollary of these signs of encouragement is open and honest expression of concerns and doubts by the tutor, such as:

'I'm a bit worried about the timing on this.'
'I'm just a bit afraid that you won't be able to get this information.'
'I'm concerned about the risk.'

This is no more than good communications practice. Expressions of concern, mixed with questions, are a powerful means of exploring and re-shaping risky or unwieldy contract proposals.

'I'm a bit worried about . . .' allows for the possibility that the proposal is perfectly achievable and the tutor is being over-anxious. Whereas:

'The timing is wrong.'

'You won't get this information.'
'The risk's too great.'

are all flat, unequivocal statements, with very little room for discussion. A tutor should be very sure of their facts before they are so blunt. Again, this is little more than good communications practice.

Review

Becoming an effective contract tutor will involve at least acquiring an understanding of the basic principles of contract learning, agreeing and carrying out a successful contract oneself and, ideally, negotiating and assessing some practice contracts with others. Negotiation is a key part of the process, and one which many professional educators and trainers may find a little alien and unusual.

We have seen that there are certain identifiable skills which are of value to negotiating learning contracts. They are based on the professional ability to evaluate learners' proposals; this will require a degree of subject knowledge or expertise in the contract field. In this chapter we have concentrated on the communication skills that are needed to help the learner to develop an effective contract.

Chapter 10

Support

Where learning contracts are used to best effect, support for the learner begins before the negotiation of the contract, in the priming and other preparatory activities we have described, and continues until after the assessment, as the learner is encouraged to think of further areas for learning and development.

In this chapter, however, we are concerned with support for the learner during the process of tackling the contract, and in particular the support that may be organized or provided by the person who has negotiated the contract with the learner – the tutor. Learners using contracts, as with other forms of flexible learning, often welcome this kind of support (Rowntree 1992). Indeed, some learners may find some form of support essential if they are to be successful. However capable and independent they may be in other aspects of their lives, the challenge of learning independently through the use of a learning contract may be too much for them without support (Brookfield 1986, Chapter 4).

Of relevance to learning contracts, Robinson (1995) notes that research in this area indicates:

1. Regular contact with the learner by tutors appears to have a positive effect on learner persistence and performance.
2. Learners value contact with tutors and other learners, although they do not always use the services which are offered. They prefer face-to-face meetings to other forms of contact.

In addition, some learners, approaching contract learning for the first time, may have a strong expectation of support – associating 'learning' with inputs, resources and help from a tutor. It is partly a matter of policy (and of resources) as to how far the programme team, and the individual tutor, are prepared to meet this expectation.

A way of examining what support might be provided is to consider the activities the learner is undertaking, and suggest how these might be supported. Cost considerations are likely to come into the equation fairly soon: for example, regular individual tutorials with a capable tutor will provide excellent support to an interested learner, but at a high price. Learning contracts can be heavily supported and heavily resourced by a programme provider. But they can also work very effectively with fewer resources, intelligently used, and the commitment of the learner.

The purpose and priorities of the programme and of using learning contracts within it must also be considered. An aim of encouraging and enhancing the skills of independent learning may be incompatible with some kinds of support activity, or with a high level of support.

Action plans

Let us first consider the action plans the learners might be tackling. The details of each plan will vary with the specific contract, of course, but we might consider the range of activities of a learner undertaking a piece of research, on the one hand, and a learner who is aiming to develop a skill or competence, on the other.

The researcher will be gathering information of various types, analysing and synthesizing it, and drafting a report or a dissertation. Possible activities are set out in Table 10.1 together with possible support activities that the tutor might organize or arrange. The support activities are a mixture of providing:

- practical information, advice and resources
- encouragement and psychological support.

There are different degrees of possible support within the brief descriptions contained in Table 10.1. 'Providing access to published materials' might range from the tutor actually providing copies of relevant materials at one, highly supportive extreme, to the lower level of support of providing suggestions as to a starting point for the research, and arranging for the learner's enrolment in a suitable library.

'Regular meetings with the tutor to discuss progress' might be regularly once every three months, or much more frequently – say once a week.

Each of the brief descriptions of supporting activities can be stretched in this way: we will look at the possible ranges for some of these categories later in the chapter.

For a learner undertaking a contract to develop skills or competences, the activities are likely to include points from various stages around the Learning Cycle such as gathering information from published sources, or from individuals, or by observation, about models of good practice, and about techniques and tactics; analysing and synthesizing this information; attending workshops or training courses to develop the skill; identifying

Table 10.1 *Research activities and possible support*

Learner activities	Possible support
Gathering information from published sources	Providing access to published materials
Interviewing, surveying people	Arranging access to people and events
Gathering information on events, e.g. by observation or measurement	
Attending relevant conferences, lectures and seminars	Arranging or providing access to lectures, seminars and conferences relevant to the topic of the research, and/or to relevant research methods
Analysing and synthesizing information	Arranging access to equipment or people to assist in gathering and analysing information
Reviewing and refining a frame of reference	Regular meetings with tutor to discuss progress
	Interim milestones and targets
	Open access available by mail and phone
	Organize meetings with other learners to discuss progress
	Organize a 'buddy' system with pairs or triads of learners
Drafting a report/dissertation	Feedback on early draft reports

opportunities for practice; practising – i.e. taking action; evaluating the level of performance. Table 10.2 sets out the possible activities together with the support that might be made available.

In Table 10.2, also, the brief descriptions may conceal a range of differences. The level and type of support may differ from contract to contract, as the actual nature of the skill development may be quite different from learner to learner, as may be the nature of the practice sessions and the underlying models of good practice.

Where the programme is a mixture of skill development and academic work, the action plan may include activities from Tables 10.1 and 10.2.

In both types of contract, some of these supporting activities can be carried out at the outset: booklists and introductions can be provided, and inputs on research methods etc. can be organized. Other types of support are activities that would take place after the contract has been going for a little while.

The structure of the programme and the length of the contract will influence the type and level of this ongoing support that can be provided. Where the contract carries on over several months, it is helpful to arrange meetings and interim milestones and targets: these give learners some psychological support at the very least. Where the learning contracts are short – under six weeks, as a watershed length – the benefits of such meetings must be carefully weighed against the costs. A telephone call – or the invitation to the learner to call the tutor if required – can provide the most cost-effective support for these short contracts. Much depends, of course, on the maturity of the learner, the clarity of the contract and the quality of the initial support.

Table 10.2   *Skills development activities and possible support*

Learner activities	Possible support
Gathering information on good practice from: published sources practitioners observation Analysing and synthesizing information	Access to: published ideas on good practice people and events to interview or observe
Attending workshops or training sessions to develop the skill	Workshops, training sessions, seminars to provide knowledge and practice pitches for development of the skill
Identifying opportunities for practice Taking action to practise and develop the skill Gathering feedback on performance Evaluating performance	Access to equipment and/or opportunities to practise the skill Feedback on performance
Confirming or modifying ideas on how to achieve good practice	Regular meetings with tutor to discuss progress Interim milestones and targets Open access available by mail and phone Organize meetings with other learners to discuss progress Organize a 'buddy' system with pairs or triads of learners
Preparing evidence – a learning log, or product evidence, etc.	Feedback on evidence

Levels of support

We have identified some possible support activities. Let us now consider what level of support might be supplied in each case.

Published information

Published information is often important to both types of contract. The actual publications could be given to the learner – or the tutor might indicate only the references of one or two starting points.

With learning contracts that frame research projects, the common practice seems to be to provide a list of the basic references for the core area(s) of knowledge nearest to the specialized area of the research, and for the tutor to then give advice (if necessary) on general direction, or likely sources. Inclusions may be indicated as the contract progresses, rather than at the outset – partly to encourage learners to carry out their own research.

With skills development contracts, tutors need to balance the benefit to the learner of providing the information against the benefit of the learner finding it out for themselves and developing their own model of good practice. The provision of a model of good practice (provided it is actually

Box 10.1 Specific directions for development

Even where people work with the same competence statement from a model, the direction and nature of their development may be different.

For example, several people have targeted the competence of Logical Thought for development, in order to improve their performance as leaders. The competence is taken from the model researched by Boyatzis (1982) and the key behaviours concern the ability to establish a cause and effect relationship between factors in an event.

Generally learners who want to develop this capability see themselves (or are seen by others) as being too intuitive, instinctive and impulsive in their thinking. They look for systematic analytical techniques they can use to organize their thinking, and try to establish the habit of using these techniques on a regular basis.

However, one learner wanted to develop this competency specifically in the area of organizational politics (i.e. he wanted to be able to be more logically analytical about the behaviours of people within his organization) which took him into a study of organizational dynamics and systems theory. Another wanted, in particular, to be able to explain matters in a more logical way. He spent extra time on identifying and considering the perspectives of his listeners, and the factors that affected these perspectives.

A number of learners have aimed to develop the self-confidence competence from the Boyatzis model. Some use a strategy of concentrating on their feelings in difficult situations, and on learning how to give themselves the right to be wrong (where appropriate); others have used almost the opposite strategy – they seek to improve their understanding of events and ideas, on an habitual basis, so that they can be confident of their facts.

a realistic one) may appear to save time, and to enable the learner to make more progress in developing the skill over the period of the contract. Leaving the learner to develop their own model may run the risk of the model being unbalanced or unrealistic (if the skill is new to the learner).

If there is a clear and agreed model for the skill (such as calculating the internal rate of return, or the net present value, on an investment, for example) or there are accepted techniques which can develop the skill (such as force field analysis for persuasion and change management skills, for example, or herring-bone analysis for establishing the causes of problems) it may be better use of the learner's time and effort for the tutor simply to indicate or to provide this material.

Where there is no single clear and agreed model (or at least no single model in which the tutor has great confidence) the best approach may be to indicate a number of possibilities that the learner might take into account, and agree that they will synthesize a realistic model of skilled behaviour. (For examples, see Boxes 6.3 and 7.1.)

It follows that tutors need to establish a bank of materials and further references to support contracts. The learner can see quick initial progress on a contract if they are able to borrow a relevant book, article, or video-tape. This can help them through the fallow time that will otherwise occur while they wait for materials they have ordered to be made available by the library or the bookshop. It is obviously very helpful for tutors to have the necessary knowledge to be able to point learners to sources of relevant information, and even to be able to make available copies of models and approaches that are in much demand.

Not all published information is paper-based, or captured on video-tape, of course. The Internet may be a valuable source of information for a learner's contract. Support may take the form of helping the learner to gain access to suitable equipment, and to learn the necessary skills to use it.

Access to equipment

Information technology is playing an increasingly significant part in the lives of those who study, and the lives of many of the workforce. As it was introduced into the geography of more and more jobs between 1986 and 1995, it was a favourite learning contract topic for many of the managers who undertook the Certificate in Management Studies in that period (see Box 2.3). Perhaps it is more likely now to be a means by which a contract is achieved and reported on than a contract subject itself.

Particular contracts may benefit from the use of a word-processing facility, and a database, a spreadsheet, and access to the Internet. In addition, electronic conferencing may be a proposed support method for a group of learners.

Again, the level of help the tutor will provide a learner to gain access to the equipment – and the skills to use it – is partly a matter of policy, and partly a matter of economics. It is likely to be feasible to provide learners with access to suitable IT equipment and to relevant training courses in larger educational institutions and corporate training departments. Where the use of IT is expected to comprise a substantial component of the pro-gramme – for example, through electronic conferencing – tutors may decide, at one extreme, to provide the equipment and training as part of the pro-gramme fees or, at the other extreme, to permit entry onto the programme only to people who can show that they have access to the necessary equip-ment and skills.

Access to people and events

Learners may need access to certain people as part of the contract.

The learner may wish to interview expert practitioners, for example, or survey a representative sample of respondents. On a sliding scale of involvement, the tutor may:

- suggest people to be contacted
- provide advice on how to contact people
- provide an introduction
- use relevant people as visiting speakers.

This final option, of using relevant people as visiting speakers, is only realistic if a number of learners will benefit from the input – and therefore depends on a degree of commonality between a number of contracts.

Learners may also seek access to certain events – to observe, or measure or compare. In a similar vein, the tutor may:

- suggest events the learner might study
- help the learner gain access to events
- provide direct access to events.

The final option – providing direct access to events – may be possible where the contract fits in with an existing research project being carried out by the tutor or the programme team. It is quite realistic for the tutor to be able to offer the lower levels of support, however, using either their academic or work-based contacts.

With work-based learning contracts, the employer may be a source of access to relevant people or events; or other learners in the group may be able to provide help in gaining access.

Access to opportunity

In skills development contracts, the opportunity to take action is a key resource. In work-based learning programmes, this type of opportunity is more often in the gift of the learner's line manager – or other managers who are in a position to allow the learner to take real action in the workplace – such as leading projects, leading meetings, making key presentations, analysing situations and making recommendations. The tutor may be able to help in this – especially if the learner is quite a junior member of the organization – by discussing the requirements with the line manager, or providing a sound general briefing on the nature of learning contracts, and by so doing paving the way for the learner to make specific requests.

The tutor may also arrange simulations and practice sessions, especially if meetings have been arranged with groups of learners.

Lectures, workshops, training sessions

Because of the individual nature of contracts it may be uneconomic for the tutor to arrange formal inputs or practice sessions of this kind specifically to support a learning contract, unless a number of learners have needs in common.

In some cases a group of learners will have obvious needs in common – for example the need to develop the appropriate research skills necessary to tackle a learning contract that frames a piece of research. Or the need to practise presentation skills, if each learner is required to carry out a formal presentation as part of the assessment of the contract. In these cases there will be a degree of relevance for all in workshops or training sessions on the relevant area(s).

Otherwise, it may be possible to link learners to other available inputs or events – relevant parts of college modules, or company training programmes – which learners can attend. There is a degree of opportunism in this, which can best be exercised if the tutor and the learner maintain a high level of awareness of possible available inputs. The length of the contract is once more a practical factor: suitable inputs are more likely to be available within the time span of a long contract than a short one.

Feedback

The tutor could possibly initiate, gather, collect or co-ordinate feedback on the learner's development.

On research projects, and in other cases when substantial reports are to be written, the tutor may arrange for partial, early drafts to be completed, and may give feedback on these.

In skills development contracts, the tutor may give personal feedback, or instigate feedback from group practice sessions. There are some obvious issues here about the extent to which the learner's level of skill is really represented in the performance seen by the tutor or by his or her colleagues, but in some cases group practice sessions may provide a rare safe area where a learner can experiment, and may actually ask for and receive honest feedback. It can be most valuable in these types of contract for the tutor to help learners to develop feedback-seeking (and feedback-giving) skills.

Meetings

Arranging meetings – with individual learners and with groups – are naturally the most common support activities. A programme which uses learning contracts may contain a mixture of:

- individual meetings with a tutor, plus the facility to contact the tutor by phone, fax, mail or e-mail
- group meetings with fellow learners, with or without a tutor in attendance.

Group meetings may be structured to take the learning experience towards an action learning approach, where the group members contribute to one another's learning and development. Group meetings can add another rich dimension to the experience of learning, marrying the individually negotiated contract objectives to collective exploration and interaction (Brookfield 1986, p 62; Revans 1980, p 16). The action learning approach requires the establishment of an accepted process of sharing, questioning, helping and supporting among group members.

Group meetings may also be a point for introducing and examining ideas and frameworks which are relevant to all (or most) of the group members, and arranging practice sessions of relevant skills. Care must be taken by the tutor to influence the desired function(s) and processes of the group meetings. Are they largely self-help groups, where the group will organize itself, create its own agendas and take its own decisions – perhaps with some facilitation from the tutor? Or will the tutor provide the main inputs into the agenda, organize what experience tells him/her will be useful expositions and exercises?

On longer programmes, tutors may want the best of both worlds – the opportunity to supply relevant inputs at the right time in the programme, and for the group members to take responsibility for their own learning. It may be difficult to make this transition without having two separate types of meetings, or without having a clear break in the one regular scheduled meeting, to signal the move from the tutor-led to the learner-led component.

Individual tutorial meetings may be scheduled to support longer contracts, together with interim milestones – targets the learner aims to meet, or tasks it is agreed that the learner will undertake.

At their best, individual discussions with a tutor, or exchanges in a group meeting, can:

- provoke reflective thinking
- help learners maintain a focus on the aims of the contract
- suggest new actions they make take, new resources they may use
- expand their understanding of ideas
- help learners to review their progress and their level of understanding or ability
- provide encouragement and refresh their commitment.

In the case of contracts to develop skills and competences, the ideal supporting discussions will help the learner round the Learning Cycle. So, supportive discussion may aim to stimulate and support the Reflector–Theorist dimension by encouraging reflection and evaluation of performance,

Box 10.2 Supporting meetings

On the flexible MBA programme first mentioned in Box 2.1, in the structure used between 1989 and 1995, learners undertook contracts of between 3 and 9 months in duration, and workshops of groups of learners were held on a monthly basis. These meetings were used for a variety of purposes – for initial priming, for the introduction and discussion of ideas and frameworks that were likely to be relevant to most of the contracts, for some needs analysis work, and for ongoing support. Attendance was voluntary, but in most cases it reflected the degree of progress and commitment of the learner: a sequence of non-attendances generally signalled that a learner was finding difficulty putting time into the programme.

Most learners welcomed interim meetings, although not all benefited from the group meetings – particularly those who were making faster than average progress.

As learners settled on their individual contracts, there was a tendency to a lack of common enterprise, and in many of the groups that were formed over the years there was no more than a limited contribution by colleagues to the work of fellow learners. There was a general tendency for group members to avoid offering challenges or constructive criticisms, and to be too gentle with one another.

The members of the group had common interests – in that they were all engaged in developing work-based skills, and in exploring a relevant body of knowledge about leadership and management, and being assessed by tutors for the award of the Master's degree. Discussions in this area generally attracted interest and comment. But once the contracts were under way, focusing on a specific skill area would only attract a limited amount of interest from learners, unless it happened to be a target of their contract.

A benefit of the meetings, however, as reported by the learners, was that they supplied regular boosts to their motivation. On a more practical note, they also provided points where the learners could step out of the task orientation of their work role – which was continually being reinforced by their colleagues in the workplace – and concentrate on the competences they were trying to develop.

the exploration of new ideas, and the synthesis of ideas into new forms. Supporting the Pragmatist–Activist dimension may involve encouraging people to develop action plans and to put them into practice.

As people have different preferences for these different activities, the support that is of most value to one learner may not be needed by another. The high-scoring Theorist needs no urging to read another book – but may

Box 10.3 Learning styles

Strong preferences for particular learning styles can have a dramatic effect on how people approach learning contracts. One learner, Steve, had strong preferences for Action and for Theory, and weak preferences for Reflection and Planning. His profile, represented in diagrammatic form, was:

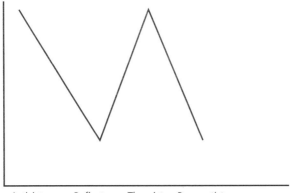

| Activist | Reflector | Theorist | Pragmatist |

This was a reasonably accurate picture of his learning behaviour: he read voraciously, and he was quick to take action; but he was poor at sifting through the ideas he had read and planning how to apply them to real life, and he was also poor at reflecting on why things hadn't worked out as he hoped, and adjusting his ideas.

He was on a learning programme that entailed a number of short contracts, with no intervening support meetings. This pattern of behaviour was very clear after the first contract he undertook. With the second and subsequent contracts, specific reference was made to the action planning and the reflection parts of the cycle at the time the contract was agreed. An interim meeting, before the contract period was completed, where questions that prompted Steve to reflect and to evaluate, would have helped him.

benefit from some agreed deadlines for when they will start to practise their new skill. The high Activist will, logically, benefit from the opposite kind of support – encouragement to reflect on the many activities undertaken, and to relate activity in a realistic way to published ideas.

The other members of the group, or the tutor, may pick up on these needs. When the contract is a complex one, people can get lost in their preferred area of learning and activity, and it can take another perspective to notice this.

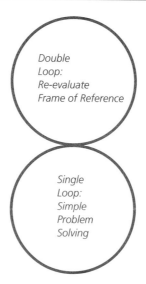

Figure 10.1   Double loop learning

Additionally, as a person goes through the learning process, they may encounter set-backs and difficulties, and periods when what they are trying to achieve seems out of reach or – worse – of doubtful worth. There may be times when they appear to have taken two steps forward and three steps back, or when an earlier estimate of their improved level of ability or understanding seems suddenly to be exposed as hopelessly optimistic. The support of colleagues at this point is usually worth more than any words a tutor can offer. It is worth recalling at these times that the learning curve is not in reality a simple shape showing a regular, measured ascent – nor that ascent is guaranteed without effort and ingenuity.

Another model of the learner's thinking processes, sometimes appropriate at difficult times, is that of double loop learning (Argyris and Schon 1978) (Figure 10.1). Rather than setting out to solve a specific problem, or simply add to our store of knowledge, or repertoire of skills – which might all be represented as simple, single loop learning – we sometimes find ourselves having to redefine the problem, reorientate deeper aspects of our under-standing, or question aspects of our capability and character we did not imagine would be touched by this learning contract.

Despite the benefits of group discussion, camaraderie and support, serious progress chasing will usually require individual tutorial discussions – unless the members of the group have been thoroughly convinced that they are collectively responsible for each member's performance, and individually responsible to the group for achieving success. This is an ideal state of action learning: in most cases, however, there is a role for a tutor to intervene and either initiate discussions or respond to requests from individual learners.

Box 10.4 Adding or transforming?

In contracts to develop skills and competences, the extent of personal development is sometimes an issue for debate.

Bill, an MBA student, was a rising star in a large chemical company. In group situations on the programme he often exhibited high Shaper behaviour – pushing, directive, task centred. For one of his learning contracts he aimed to enhance his leadership ability by developing a less directive approach. By the end of the nine-month contract period, he was able to show examples of his new approach to leadership, as well as a convincing understanding of the theoretical underpinnings of the area. Asked by an examiner at his penultimate oral presentation whether this learning represented a transformation of his natural approach to leadership, he said after some thought that it was instead another weapon in his armoury, and that his first inclination was still to use directive approaches to leading others.

A second senior manager who undertook the MBA programme some years after Bill aimed for a similar change in his leadership style. Over the period of the contract, he developed a pattern of behaving in a facilitative, supporting style with his team of managers. By establishing this pattern of behaviour within this (relatively) stable group, he perhaps came closer to transforming his 'natural' – i.e. instinctive – style than Bill had done, and had perhaps done more than simply add another weapon to his armoury.

This role is particularly important when the programme leads to a qualification, for the tutor then has additional responsibilities in relation to assessment.

Review

We have surveyed a number of possible types and levels of support that tutors can provide for learners who are undertaking contracts. There is no doubt that, particularly with contracts of longer than six weeks in duration, most learners welcome the opportunity to meet a tutor and a group of fellow learners and discuss progress, and that this degree of support can enhance the effectiveness of the contract.

Similarly, some guidance on useful reading, at the outset of the contract in particular, can help the learner make quick initial progress, and enhance their motivation.

The ability and willingness of the tutor, and of the programme team, to supply other types of support during the contract will depend on the:

- nature of the contract
- resources available to the team
- extent to which the philosophy of self-managed learning is central to the programme.

The lack of a key resource – access to a suitable computer, for example, or the opportunity to develop skills by leading a project – may simply mean that the learner must re-think their contract proposal, and work within the resources that are available.

Ongoing meetings during a contract can add a rich element to the learning itself, and can provide good opportunities to review progress and prepare for the final assessment. The following chapter considers the issues and practices of carrying out assessment of the contract at these interim and final stages.

Chapter 11

Assessment

The importance of assessment has been noted at various points throughout this book. Assessment lends an immediacy to a learning contract, and provides a precise set of targets for the learner to hit. If the learning contract has been negotiated properly, then assessment should not present too many problems.

In this respect assessment tests the learning contract and the tutor almost as much as the learner. The tutor finds out not only about the learner's progress, but also about his/her own level of skill in negotiating effective learning contracts, and the evidence that is produced for assessment is also likely to be used by the programme team to evaluate the contribution of the learning contract approach to the programme.

Of course, when the learning contract contributes to the award of a qualification, the outcome of the assessment has another dimension of consequence for the learner, and the process of assessment is generally more formal, more subject to procedures and regulations.

In Chapter 8 we discussed the design and negotiation of assessment measures at the outset of a learning contract. In this chapter we consider some of the practices and issues in the evaluation of completed contracts.

The assessment process

Naturally, assessment processes vary, depending on the programme.

In many cases, where the programme leads to a qualification, the tutor will read a written report the learner has produced, making judgements about its quality, and provide a grade and written comments. In some cases, an oral presentation, or an interview, may be part of the assessment process. In fact, on non-qualification programmes this oral approach is likely to be the main medium of assessment. Where the contract aims to develop skills, the evidence may also include a demonstration of the skill by the learner, or the testimony of people who have witnessed the learner's actions, or other corroborating material (NCVQ 1995).

With longer learning contracts, the final (or *summative*) assessment may be preceded by some interim (or *formative*) assessment of work in progress, which will include feedback to the learner on the quality of the work produced to date. This interim evaluation and feedback is part of the learning process.

Tutors working with learning contracts – in common with tutors who are supervising any assessed research project – need to agree on the boundaries between interim and final assessment, and on the extent to which it is legitimate to guide the learner in the later stages of the contract. On some programmes summative assessment is a significant stage, because the learner may only be allowed a limited number of submissions before they are deemed to have failed the contract, or the module, or the programme.

Programme regulations may require summative assessment by more than one tutor. They may stipulate 'second marking' by a colleague, or by an external examiner, or an internal or external verifier, to ensure quality control. The regulations may also reserve the authority to make the final decision about the acceptability of the contract to a formal committee or examination board. There are some obvious benefits in involving other assessors. The quality of the evidence is assured. An external perspective, and a balanced evaluation, can inform decisions about future practice. Quality assurance of this nature – and the practical benefits it brings – can also be good for the reputation of the programme and of the learning contract approach.

However, these formal processes all take time, and delay the assessment decision. From the learner's viewpoint, the contract process, which has been flexible and responsive to this point, may now appear slow and bureaucratic. Different tutors may also bring different baggage to the assessment: this can be helpful where it enriches the programme, but problematic when diverse priorities lie outside the original vision of the programme and of the learning contract. This is a problem most keenly felt on the first occasion learning contracts are used – on the pilot programme – where assessment policies and standards are still being developed, and the first line tutor is likely to be less confident that his/her evaluation will reflect those of the other assessors.

On all programmes – whether or not they include learning contracts – assessment policies and standards are normally developed:

1. In advance of the programme launch.
2. On a case-by-case basis, as the programme proceeds.

The pilot group of learners on a programme are likely to give rise to considerable case law and precedent. On pilot programmes it is advisable to adopt the following procedures.

• Move the pilot group swiftly through the assessment process, organizing a quicker path through second marking and external assessment than will later be the norm, and arrange for frequent meetings and discussions among assessors – to make sure that all involved in assessment have a broad agreement on standards, and to develop policy in any grey areas.

• Agree a position on precedents that does not unduly penalize the pilot group of learners. For example, borderline case learner A may be passed as complete by the first and second internal markers; some weeks later, the external examiner (or verifier) may express doubts about the quality of the evidence in this case. In future – it is agreed – evidence of this standard will not be counted as satisfactory: but the decision of the internal assessors in learner A's case is allowed to stand. This is a pragmatic rule, to help learners and tutors manage the extra uncertainty that surrounds a pilot programme. Its application may depend in part on how far short of the standard learner A is deemed to fall: it may not be agreed to apply in the case of complete failure learner B, who has somehow also passed successfully through the internal system (Boak 1995).

Outcomes of assessment

At first, second, or third marking, the possible outcomes of the assessment of a learning contract may be:

1. The evidence is judged to meet the terms agreed for the contract, and any other standards that apply, and the contract is assessed as complete.

2. The evidence fails to meet the explicit terms agreed for the contract, but it is still assessed as complete. This may be the verdict on those occasions when the targets in the contract have been substantially achieved, and with hindsight it is realized that the original contract was unrealistic, or too large.

3. The evidence does not meet the original terms, or some of the other standards that apply, and the learner is required to carry out additional work to complete the contract, as agreed in the original proposal. It may be that the learner has overlooked some parts of the original proposal, or misinterpreted what was required, or has simply been unable to complete what was required in time.

4. The evidence does not meet the original terms agreed for the contract, and additional work is required – but the contract is in effect partially re-negotiated to specify the extra work that is required. This may be appropriate to take account of changing circumstances, where the original proposal is no longer practical. Indeed, it may be that changing circumstances have led to the shortfall in the evidence. In an ideal

world, such contracts are re-negotiated when the problem first becomes apparent, but sometimes learners let the matter slide until the time comes to assess the contract.

Whether or not the contract is graded depends in part on the programme regulations – some form of grading may be required. Grading the work that results from learning contracts is often more difficult than grading other course work – because of the individual nature of the contracts there is less scope for comparison with the work of other learners. Grading is also often seen as antithetical to the work-based and competence-based programmes where contracts are often used – as well as being difficult to justify in these types of programmes (but see Wolf 1994). However, grading – even using only a few broad bands – is helpful in sending signals to the learner, and also in enabling compensation or aggregation between contracts and/or other assessments, and the programme team is well advised to weigh these advantages and disadvantages carefully in their own situation.

The standard of assessment

The standard against which the contract is assessed will depend on what has been agreed explicitly between the tutor and the learner, and on the programme in which the contract is located. This standard may be, in part, fixed and, in part, relative to the learner's entry behaviour.

Where the contract forms part of a qualification, the learner's performance may be measured against a standard associated with the level of the programme. If the contract is truly a *learning* contract, then some evidence of learning should also be apparent. These two factors may be combined in the assessment of a contract – or one or the other may predominate. For example, on one MBA programme (first described in Box 2.1) learners were expected to demonstrate:

* their development in key selected competences
* a good understanding of the subject area, commensurate with the level of the qualification.

They were not expected to be excellent performers (however that may be defined) in their targeted competency areas. This probably encouraged them to concentrate on areas where they needed to develop, rather than leading them to choose target areas where they were already strong (although this was a choice they were free to make). At the end of the contract, they were required to show some development had been achieved, and it was expected that the targeted competence area would no longer be a deficiency – although it may not (yet) be a strength.

The main area where the minimum standard applied was in the more academic and intellectual realm of relating the competence to an accepted body of knowledge.

On the other hand, in another postgraduate Diploma programme (outlined in Figure 3.6) the only requirement in respect of the long learning contract is that the learners show some learning and development. Other assessments on the programme are anchored to the academic standards that generally apply at that level of qualification.

As a third example, in the UK, in some National and Scottish Vocational Qualification programmes, 'learning contracts' are used to agree the specific evidence a candidate will present for assessment. In these cases the evidence is measured against the Occupational Standards, which contain the criteria for assessment. The candidate may or may not engage in learning in order to produce the evidence – they may simply be proving that they already meet the required standard. There are advantages to the candidate in this, but this is hardly a *learning* contract.

On the Master's programme, learners are required to show some degree of development, however capable they might be of achieving a required standard. Assessment is thus not only of the level of the learner's understanding or skill at the end of the contract, but the extent to which this represents a development on their level of skill or knowledge at the beginning.

Trade-offs

We have already seen that learning contracts can involve a number of trade-offs:

> *People will be highly motivated to learn, but they may not want to learn what we think they* should *learn.*

This is a basic paradox of the learning contract approach. As a tutor, sometimes you can exert a little positive influence over the direction of the contract, sometimes you can help the learner avoid a danger or an obstacle that lies in their proposed path, but most times your job is to help the learner do whatever they want to do.

A second apparent conundrum, a topic for discussion at the assessment stage, is that by the use of learning contracts:

> *People can become more effective self-directed learners, but they may not learn as much as they would if they were taught by an expert.*

In other words, the standard they achieve at the end of the contract – at the time of assessment – may appear lower that we might expect if they had been given expert tuition.

Is this true? In some cases, yes, but with qualifications. First, it may be true for subject-based learning. If I am, say, a social science undergraduate using a learning contract to structure a research project, I may well emerge from the project six months later knowing less about the object of my study than if I had been taught about it over the same period by an expert. However, I am almost certainly less dependent on experts at the end of my contract than I would be if I had relied on their tuition throughout the period. The lower standard in the subject-related learning may be acceptable in the light of the development in my skills of self-directed learning.

Secondly, the case is hypothetical, unless there exists an expert who can provide the tuition. This is an issue partly of expertise and partly of economics. Is there an expert in the subject area? Can an expert be provided, at a reasonable cost, for each area that learners wish to cover? If the answers to these questions is in the affirmative, then in the short term it makes good sense to provide that expert. But the expert may not be available at a reasonable cost, or a main part of the agenda may lie in developing the learning skills of the individual.

A further trade-off may apply where learning contracts are used to help people develop skills and competences in the context of an academic qualification. Learners spend time and effort developing the skills and competences that they would otherwise have spent on developing their theoretical understanding of the area. When they come to be assessed, they have a lower theoretical understanding, but a higher level of practical ability (Figure 11.1).

This trade-off can give rise to serious debates about the aims of the programme and the standards implied by particular levels of qualification, and it is an area where a programme team must reach at least some broad agreement on what they expect the learners to be able to demonstrate at the end of their learning contracts, and at the end of the programme.

To summarize, in the context of a programme leading to a qualification, the questions are to what extent can:

- theoretical understanding be traded off against increased ability in the application?
- learning of the subject be traded off against increased independent learning skills?
- direction of learning be traded off against increased motivation and commitment?

The programme team will probably debate the acceptable parameters – both in advance of the first assessments and then as individual cases arise.

The reflective report

Reflective reports are a useful and common form of evidence for assessing learning contracts. For contracts which aim to develop complex skills, the

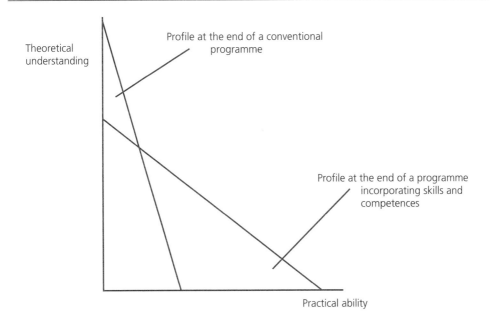

Figure 11.1 Trade-offs between growth in practical ability and growth in theoretical understanding

report will be a principal piece of evidence. A reflective report can be seen as a means of crystallizing and sharing the learner's experiences and his/her evaluation of them. Preparing the report – and receiving feedback on it during formative assessment – is often in itself a valuable part of the learning process, rather than something which is undertaken after the learning has finished.

Reflective reports are often simply developments of learning logs, or learning journals, where people note key events and their reflections on them (Honey 1989; Pedler *et al.* 1986, Activity 6). The value of reflective reportage is partly based on, and supported by, ideas about how professionals best acquire skills (Schon 1983, 1991).

Learners new to reflective reportage generally experience some initial difficulties in producing them, however, and benefit from structure, guidance and feedback.

The stages of the Learning Cycle can provide a useful structure for reflective reports, i.e.

Planning – the learner sets out what they aimed to achieve in the contract.

Action – they describe what they did in a situation (or a number of situations). Depending on the size and scope of the contract, the report may contain a number of events. In some events, the action may be described in detail – this can be particularly important when the contract is aimed at

---

Box 11.1 Writing about development

Learners can find it difficult to explain the development of their skills and competences in writing. The following points are sometimes useful for their guidance:

- development of a skill or a competence will be shown by several examples of behaviour

This encourages learners to provide a sufficient number of examples, rather than just one or two.

- development of a skill or competence will be shown by comparison with behaviour prior to the learning contract

This encourages learners to make an explicit comparison between before and after.

- development of a skill or competence will be indicated by some description of the efforts the learner made to improve.

This encourages learners to provide some account of what actions they took in order to develop.

---

improving some aspect of process skills, or when the contract included certain crucial events – such as a big presentation or a key meeting. For larger contracts, where the report covers actions that take place over several weeks or months, the report needs to provide a clear, brief overview of what happened, as well as a detailed account of some key events.

Reflection – the learner provides an evaluation of their behaviour, in terms of its effectiveness, and in terms of the extent to which it showed a development of their skills.

Theory – they link their behaviour to theories and principles of performance; they modify and synthesize these theories to fit their own context; they develop rules of thumb on the basis of their experience. Where the contract is part of a higher-level academic qualification, the ability to link behaviour to relevant published ideas will be an important part of the assessment.

Planning – they set out action plans for what they will do next, beyond the time frame of the contract. Learning contracts, by their nature, are focused on limited, specific improvements in skill and knowledge within a particular period of time. Including a further action plan as part of the assessment stage is another way of getting the learner to evaluate the extent of their development. It can also be a means of generating and maintaining forward momentum, so that all learning and development does not cease when the contract is judged to be complete.

The above structure is not rigid, and where a number of actions are described it is usually most effective to have a series of short action–reflection–theory loops in the account, rather than a description of *all* the action, followed by a description of *all* the reflection, and then a section comprising *all* the relevant theory. A final review and summing up is usually valuable.

Reflective reports can favour those learners with well-honed writing skills, and penalize those who have more difficulty in this area, and so the accuracy of the assessment may be distorted by the learner's level of written skills. This is a drawback of the medium, and assessors are well advised to be watchful for those who may be unfairly helped or hindered in this respect. An oral report from the learner or an interview can often add great value to what has been written, as well as allowing assessors to probe the learner's account.

Weighing the evidence

With the increase in provision of work-based learning, there are a number of different formulations of the general criteria that can be used to evaluate the evidence of completion of a contract (for example, NCVQ 1995; TDLB 1995; Beaumont 1995; Wolf 1994; Mitchell and Bartram 1994, Chapter 3; Lee 1994; Caple and Mitchell 1992). We shall concentrate on three. Evidence – of whatever kind – should be:

- *valid*: it should relate to the objectives and assessment measures specified in the contract
- *authentic*: it should be genuine
- *reliable*: it should be reasonably representative of the learner's capability.

Validity

The evidence produced should relate to the relevant objectives and standards. The standards may be expressed explicitly in the contract, or may be required by the level of the programme. These standards may not be thoroughly understood by learners who, simply through inexperience, may be unsure about the match between what they have produced and the required standard.

On higher-level academic programmes, for example, there is a difference between on the one hand simply summarizing key writers and on the other engaging in the substance of the available published material, exploring the application of global ideas to local reality, examining disagreements and contradictions, and synthesizing material from two or more sources. It is easy to describe the difference between these two extremes of engagement with the material and to communicate them to learners. Experienced assessors will usually find it relatively easy to reach agreement on finer degrees of quality, but it is more difficult to explain these to learners. Rather than spelling out these standards in great detail, the quality of the evidence may simply be referenced to the judgement of an experienced assessor (Knowles 1986, pp 68–69).

The assessor's questions are simply: has all the evidence specified in the contract been produced? Does it meet the required standards?

In some aspects of validity, the learner and the assessor must beware the pitfalls of false logic. On a work-based programme, the line manager who testifies that the learner 'has worked very hard' has of course not said anything (yet) about what this hard work has produced.

On the same type of programme, the learners who report on ultimate outcomes such as:

'sales have increased'
'the project was successful'
'my proposal was accepted'

still need to show some links between these business results and their own learning.

Authenticity

Evaluating the authenticity of evidence is a second concern which has always been prominent in assessment. One of the few advantages of formal written examinations is that the papers submitted at the end of three hours are demonstrably the work of the candidates in the examination room. There is always the logical possibility that any other written work could have been produced by the candidate's smarter friends and relatives, or copied from another source.

In assessing the development of skills a similar calculus applies. Where the skill can be exhibited directly to the assessor – such as by the candidate demonstrating the skilled use of a piece of equipment – its authenticity cannot be in doubt. More complex skills and competences are much more difficult to assess. The vocational qualification movement in the UK is wary of the unsupported assertion of learners and this has led to a hunt for corroborative evidence, through the testimony of witnesses and supporting papers.

The detail and internal logic of the learner's own account can be a key factor in judging authenticity. The opportunity for questioning provided by an oral presentation and an interview can also serve to confirm – or place in doubt – the case the learner has made in a written report. Questioning

---

Box 11.2 Assessing competences in context

On competence-based programmes in particular, it can be vitally important that evidence be assessed in context, and that assessors are very clear about what is required.

One of the McBer competences is the Use of Oral Presentations (UOP), which is defined as speaking clearly and convincingly to others and maintaining the attention of the audience or listeners (Boyatzis 1982). This is an important competence in the context of using oral presentations to convince others of the virtues of a scheme or proposal.

Learners sometimes lose track of the exact target in the course of undertaking a contract. Improvement in the use of oral presentations *per se* – in a simple information-giving, or a training context – is not likely to improve the learner's performance as a manager.

Similarly the competence of Conceptualization – which is in essence the facility to identify significant patterns in events or information – can be interpreted by the learner in a technical context: so the engineer aims to improve his (already well-developed) skills at analysing engineering data. This is unlikely to improve his skill as a manager.

---

can allow the assessors to probe the learner's understanding of key ideas, or check on claims that have been made in writing.

In skills development contracts, the presentation itself can sometimes provide key items of evidence. For example, one learner claimed to have improved his drive, self-confidence and leadership capability through his learning contract, to the extent that he now took on the 'Shaper' role – that of a forceful and directive leader (Belbin 1993) – in group meetings. Among other things, he claimed to be able to make clearer and more authoritative presentations of his point of view. These claims were significantly undermined, however, by a weak and hesitant oral presentation.

The reverse of this situation can also occur – when claims that seem ambitious on paper are supported by the presence of the learner and the confident and competent way in which they present their case and respond to questions and challenges.

On work-based skills development contracts, corroboration is sometimes sought from people who have seen the learner in action. In including the testimony of these witnesses in the assessment of a learning contract, it is advisable to bear in mind some realistic limits of authenticity.

- The capability of the witness must be taken into account when weighing the value of the testimony. For example, one learner on a work-based programme collected feedback on her ability to lead meetings. The comments were favourable and the scores high – but the witnesses were

---

Box 11.3 Using witnesses: the governors

Neil based his learning contract on a work-based project. Access points to the network for distributing gas in the area, called governors, had been established in a piecemeal fashion over the years. Only the operator-engineers knew where all the governors were located. In certain circumstances it was important to be able to access the network quickly, and Neil thought that in the longer term a guide-book and record of the governors would be necessary.

His learning objectives concerned acquiring an accurate knowledge of the locations of all the governors in his area, and developing his skills in communication through the preparation of a clear and simple guide.

The clarity and simplicity of the guide, which contained photographs of the locations of all the governors, was evident. The tutor was in no position to assess the accuracy of the contents, however, nor was anyone else – except the operator-engineers, who worked for Neil.

One of the engineers attended part of the assessment. Rather than ask for his opinions on the guide, the tutor first asked him about the governors and his experience of maintaining and visiting them, and recent examples of the need to gain access to them. This enabled him to compile a list of seven or eight governors, which he was able to find set out in the guide. He then moved on to ask for opinions: did the engineer think the guide was complete? Was it useful? And so on.*

The probe for factual information, against which to check the accuracy of the learner's report, provided a better check than simply a straightforward request for an opinion.

*Note. Of course the engineer said the guide was no use to him, personally, because he already knew where all the governors were.

---

all quite young and inexperienced, and had taken part in very few meetings other than those led by the learner.

- The relationship between the witness and the learner should be borne in mind when considering witness testimony: it will be putting too much pressure on subordinates to expect them to provide absolutely truthful testimony which would result in their boss failing a learning contract, and the same may also be said of colleagues and bosses.

A final aspect of authenticity is that the learner may be tempted to overstate their initial lack of skill at the outset of the contract, in order to be sure to show some development at the assessment stage. In my experience, this has not been particularly common, nor has it been extreme – the cases have been of exaggeration rather than deliberate falsehood – and the temptation has tended to strike the learner towards the end of the contract, when they are making their case for successful completion, rather than at the outset.

In theory, it is possible for a learner to claim a lack of skill in an area where they are already proficient, and then reveal their ability in stages as the time period for the contract unfolds, but probing questions at the negotiating, supporting and assessing stages would, in practice, usually uncover such a fraud. Where the learner has willingly entered onto the programme, and has an opportunity through a learning contract to explore an area of their choice, with the offer of support and guidance, a pretence of learning planned from the outset would in any case be a cynical and wasteful exercise.

Part of the exaggeration at the assessment stage may be that learners still experience some difficulty in describing the different levels of skill (or knowledge – but degrees of skill are usually more difficult to define) by which they might explain the learning they have achieved. For example, one learner – an effective senior manager in a large corporation – reported that through his learning contract he was now 'applying concepts to reality for the first time' – an incredible claim. In fact his achievement could have been more accurately described as 'successfully applying models of personality in a systematic fashion to anticipate and explain the reactions of his work colleagues' – evidently for the first time.

Reliability

A third factor is the reliability of the evidence in accurately representing the learner's level of ability. This has always been an assessment issue. Ever since the first written examination, there have been students who have been lucky or unlucky with the questions they have found on the paper.

If the evidence is thin, or contradictory, assessors may have doubts about the true capability of the learner. For example, one learner, Ian, claimed to have made significant progress in the use of metaphor as an aid to better communication. However, in his thirty-minute oral presentation at the end of the contract, he used only one metaphor. Another (highly intelligent) learner, Jane, claimed to have improved her ability to communicate complex ideas in a clear and simple manner. Her final rehearsal of her oral presentation, however, demonstrated the familiar failing of over-complexity. Fortunately, her presentation at the summative assessment epitomized and supported the claims she had made in her written report, and convinced the assessors that she had achieved the targets set out in her contract.

Reliability in this sense shades into authenticity. There may be some question of the authenticity of Ian's claims. In Jane's case, the capability was undoubtedly present – she was able to demonstrate the skill, but not consistently.

Reliability is not an issue for debate when the assessment is a form of regulated test – such as a written examination or a demonstration. The learner takes the test and either passes or fails. The assessors are saved from pondering whether the learner's performance was typical or exceptional – at least until they consider whether they should reform the methods of assessment. But when the learning contract is aimed at improving an ongoing skill, the evidence produced by individual candidates may lead to debates within the programme team. How many examples of effective performance are required in order to demonstrate capability? Or, alternatively, what proportion of regular performance should be at the required standard? (Boyatzis 1993). A frequent request from assessors is for the learner to provide another example, or a little more information.

Review

In this chapter we have touched on some of the issues relevant to carrying out assessment.

Assessment is an important stage for all learning contracts – particularly when successful completion of the contract will lead to a qualification. In such circumstances, standards for assessment and assessment procedures should be specified as clearly as possible. However, learning contracts are unlikely to include explicit descriptions of all the standards against which they are assessed: some are inevitably implied by the level of the qualification to which they lead, and in practice the judgement and experience of the assessors will play a major role in determining whether these standards have been met.

On most qualification programmes, as a quality assurance procedure, more than one assessor will be involved in evaluating the contract, and assessment standards will be the result of debate and agreement. Where learning contracts are being used for the first time, it is advisable to make special arrangements for all the relevant parties to examine the learner's evidence more quickly than will later be normal procedure, to establish the agreed standards, and to provide more certainty for learners and first-line tutors.

The learner's evidence is weighed and evaluated by the assessors. Key concerns may be its validity, its authenticity and its reliability. For further reading on these issues, tutors who are using learning contracts in the context of work-based skills development may be interested in some of the considerable amount of work that has been done on the assessment of higher-level vocational competences – for example, NCVQ 1995; TDLB 1995; Beaumont 1995; Wolf 1994; Mitchell and Bartram 1994; Lee 1994; Eraut 1994; Caple and Mitchell 1992.

Chapter 12

Three-way contracts

So far we have discussed contracts negotiated between a learner and a tutor, in a dyadic relationship. In this chapter we consider some of the extra issues involved in three-way agreements, common in work-based learning, where a representative of the learner's employer may take part in the agreement, support and assessment of the contract. This role is often played by the learner's line manager – but a member of the company's training or personnel department may play the part instead, or there may be an in-company mentor who is neither the learner's line manager nor from the training department.

Of course, in some circumstances the primary parties to the learning contract may be the learner and their line manager – when the contract is agreed as part of the appraisal or personal development system – and the tutor or trainer is invited into the relationship in order to provide advice or support. This situation is discussed briefly at the end of this chapter. Most of what follows concerns involving the line manager, as the primary representative of the employer, as a third party to the contract.

Line manager involvement can be extremely advantageous in a number of ways, although it is not without its pitfalls. This chapter explores the advantages, the potential problems, and how the parties can work together to make the most of the partnership.

Contributions

As we saw in Chapter 2, learning contracts can bring together the three parties who are affected by any training and development, but who seldom actually work together in partnership, in an explicit learning triangle.

Ideally, the employer's representative will bring to the learning contract contributions which neither the tutor nor the learner can provide. The learner's line manager may be able to make available:

- advice on training and development needs
- advice on the realism of proposals
- learning opportunities
- ongoing support
- assistance in assessment

as well as immediate recognition of the achievements of the individual learner. This wealth of contribution can greatly enhance the value of the learning experience.

Let us examine each of these points in a little more depth.

Training and development needs

The initiative in proposing a learning contract should come from the learner, as we have seen. The advice of the line manager can be very valuable in clarifying the training needs and standards which the learner should aim to achieve. Between them, the learner and his or her boss should have a better picture of short- to middle-term development needs than anyone else, particularly when they work closely or regularly together, and when the development and assessment of subordinates is an explicit expectation within the company – through appraisal or staff development schemes.

Even where this degree of closeness or volume of information is not available, it can be helpful for the learner to receive constructive opinions from a more senior manager about development needs.

Advice on realism

Whereas a learner may be overly optimistic about the ease with which he/ she can gain access to information, or set up activities to progress the learning contract, the line manager may have a more grounded view. This of course relies upon:

- greater experience of managing people, of organizational politics and the operations of the system – this may not always apply
- more complete knowledge of plans for the future which will affect learning opportunities – this will usually hold true.

Providing learning opportunities

The line manager may actively assist the action plan by making available learning opportunities – establishing circumstances where the learner can practise a skill or obtain certain information. This is a valuable contribution of a sort the tutor is unlikely to be able to provide. Common examples include: the opportunity to carry out recruitment interviews, to present reports to committees, to take a lead role in representing the section/department at meetings, to lead teambuilding exercises, to lead change projects.

Ongoing support

As we have seen in Chapter 10, as the learning contract progresses, the learner may welcome the availability of someone who will discuss progress or problems, and who shows an interest in the outcome of his or her efforts. The line manager may be a valuable provider of this support, particularly if they can offer advice, or can empathize with the learner.

The line manager is best positioned, of all the learner's potential supporters, to cushion the possible harmful effects of changes in the workload, or circumstances that arise after the learning contract has been agreed and threaten its successful completion, and also best positioned to allow or encourage the learner to take advantage of favourable opportunities that arise – the extra meeting to be chaired, the extra negotiation to undertake, and so on. The line manager may also provide a degree of protection, or political support, if a learner's activities are opposed within the company.

Assessment

We have already acknowledged that certain aspects of improved competence are difficult for a tutor or other outside assessor to evaluate. The line manager may be in a good position to:

- testify to improved performance in a range of difficult areas, from self-organization to interpersonal skills
- testify to the accuracy of a description or analysis provided by the learner as part of the learning contract.

Summary

The line manager can play a very useful role in establishing, supporting and assessing the learning contract. The benefits to the line manager are the numerous opportunities to influence the shape and form of the training and development his or her subordinates are undertaking, such that it is relevant and useful to the needs of the job. Where this is achieved, and the individual is successful, the recognition of this success by the line manager is also valuable, rewarding and motivating the individual in a way that success on closed training and development courses may fail to do.

Box 12.1 The learning triangle

On programmes for supervisors, junior managers and aspiring managers, learning contracts have often appeared to benefit from the involvement of the learner's line manager directly in the negotiation of the contract (but see the points in Box 12.2). In these cases the line manager has often been in the meetings where the contract is first agreed and then later on assessed.

It has been more difficult to reach the same accommodation when the learners are more senior managers or highly placed professionals. To begin with, learners at higher levels in an organization usually experience more day-to-day autonomy, and may therefore have a more remote relationship with their line manager than at lower levels. This may mean they have more access to resources that can be used for learning and development, and also that their line manager may not be able to contribute so many insights about their development needs or about broader organizational issues. Secondly, there may be more resistance – or discomfort – to acknowledging a power relationship in a development context at a higher level within the organization than at a lower level. Thirdly, on a matter of simple logistics, it is often more difficult to arrange a meeting with more senior line managers, because of the pressures on their time, although they may be active in helping the learner.

Finally, if the line manager can be of assistance, more senior learners often possess the force and fluency to explain the contract process and gain involvement from the line manager, and so a discussion between tutor and line manager is less important.

Potential problems of involvement

For all the helpful contributions the line manager can bring to the contract, there are also dangers and potential problems. These need to be recognized in order to avoid, manage or minimize them. It is useful to recognize that line managers often have mixed feelings about training and development activities. They may subscribe to development as an activity to be desired, but they are usually under operational pressures to get the job done, and they will transmit these pressures to their staff, too.

Box 12.2 The value of line manager involvement

Thompson's survey of learners who had undertaken either a CMS or an MBA programme indicates a low–average level of involvement by line managers.

In the survey, learners on both programmes attributed significantly less influence to the line manager than to the tutor in the needs analysis stage of the learning contract and in its assessment (Thompson 1994 pp 64–65).

Encouragement from the line manager was not rated as a high motivational factor by respondents: for the more senior learners it was rated as the lowest of nine potential motivational factors; and it was seventh lowest for the more junior learners. Highest for both groups was 'personal growth', closely followed by 'proving one's ability' (op. cit. pp 75–76).

This may be a case where an average score conceals a wide diversity of opinion. In my experience, line manager involvement is sometimes positive and extensive, sometimes faint and peripheral, and sometimes, to a certain degree, negative.

Absentees

Some line managers may simply avoid contact, for any of a number of reasons. They may consider training and development a waste of time, or something that trainers and colleges are paid to do. They may be extremely task orientated and have little skill in people management. They may simply be extremely busy, unable to meet the tutor and the learner at a convenient time.

The action a tutor can take will depend in part on the circumstances. A clear briefing to line managers about the extent of their role may alleviate some of the fears that can lead to absenteeism. Diary dates for meetings established well in advance may catch some of the line managers with full schedules. Some line managers may miss meetings with the tutor, but play a positive and active part in supporting the learner. In the last analysis, some line managers are perhaps best missed out, and perhaps another person can be found to act as a mentor.

Project orientation

Some line managers may be inclined to see the learning contract as a way of getting a particular task done. In some cases, the requirements of the contract may be genuinely mistaken for a project – such as the one the line manager carried out in the past, on a more traditional course of education or training. This may be accompanied by an emphasis on short-term needs.

Again the solution lies in an adequate briefing about the aims and nature of the learning contracts, and the prompt use of reminders if the line manager lapses back into a project orientation during the discussions.

Domination

By far the biggest potential danger in involving the line manager in the learning contract process is that he/she may take ownership of the contract away from the learner. Some learners in these circumstances will gratefully relinquish this troublesome responsibility, and gladly do what they're told: this is probably the character of their natural working relationship with their boss, after all. In marginal cases this tendency to domination can be avoided by a clear briefing to the line managers about the importance of the learner owning the learning contract. Even with clear briefings, however, there will be occasions when the tutor has to deal with a dominant manager in the negotiation.

Some dominating line managers take a nurturing approach: protective and parental, they can help a learner to develop by giving helpful advice on apparent needs, and by making opportunities available. The danger is that there may be a reluctance to let go and allow the learner to make independent decisions. In the shorter term, the immediate problem may lie in a protective attitude towards the learner when the learning contract is assessed, and the tutor needs to be wary of their opinions and expressions of satisfaction. In addition to their natural instincts of protection, they may have become so involved in initiating and shaping the contract that they feel a sense of ownership for it, and this inclines them to be lenient in their assessments.

Alternatively, some dominant line managers are strongly orientated towards the task, the project, the needs of the department. They do not encourage a learner to explore and discuss skill developments. In the contract negotiation, they need to be discouraged from seeking short-term, task-related benefits on every occasion.

Limited skill

On some occasions the learner may propose a learning contract in an area where the line manager is not competent. Where the line manager recognizes this, the immediate danger – usually a remote one – is of unduly hurting his/her feelings or sense of self-esteem. The problem may become one of the line manager attempting to exert undue influence, as in the previous section, to steer the learner away from an area which they undervalue because of their ignorance of it.

The greater danger arises in those cases where the line manager is not competent and is unaware of this. In its extreme forms this is rare – although there may more often be an unvoiced difference of opinion between tutor and line manager as to their relative degrees of expertise. It is important for the tutor here to ensure that he or she supplies appropriate models and resources to the learner, and that assessment does not rely on the opinion of the line manager to any significant extent.

It is often helpful to clarify the limits of expertise that are expected from the line manager: to be explicit that, for example, they are not expected to be experts in the different specialized subject areas that the learners may be studying, or in the use of the competence models that the learners are using. (And if they are experts, then this is a bonus.) But their contribution may lie in their extra experience, their greater understanding of practical issues in the organization, and simply in providing a sounding board for some of the learner's ideas.

Collusion

A different kind of assessment problem may arise when the line manager feels drawn closely to the learner's side of the partnership. Such an align-ment can be quite natural. The two people work together and see each other on a regular basis: the tutor is just a visitor. In some cases the line manager, whatever his or her feelings about the results of the learning contract, will adopt a protective stance towards the learner.

If the tutor is successful in shaping the attitudes of the line manager in the briefing prior to involvement in the learning contract, some problems of collusion can be avoided, but there is no room for complacency about the success of preventive measures. Specific solutions are set out below.

Confidentiality

The involvement of the manager in the learning contract process can intro-duce new information and new opportunities, but it can also be restrictive. Learners do not always feel they can discuss their development needs with their boss. Sometimes this is because of the boss's attitudes, sometimes because of the particular need in question. (It is not unusual, for example, for a learner to analyse their difficulties in managing their time and find that a prime factor is the behaviour of their boss.)

A learner may be restricted, or feel unwilling to express a particular development need, because of the role designed for the line manager in the learning contract process. This is truly a cost of the line manager's involvement. It may be justified by reference to the many good learning contracts agreed with the help of line managers. Any hardship it causes may be eased by creating opportunities for the restricted individual to discuss their problem with the tutor or with fellow learners. A chosen mentor might even be used, as part of the design of the scheme, to avoid such a cost being incurred.

Summary

There is little point in engaging line managers of learners in negotiating and assessing learning contracts without being aware of the possible problems. Some of the dangers can be avoided, or their effects minimized, by a careful pre-briefing, and some can be combated in the negotiations and assessments themselves. We shall consider how to do this later in the chapter.

The ease or difficulty with which line managers can be engaged in any particular scheme is unpredictable – even when the programme is commissioned and paid for by the learner's employer. Experience shows that the best policy is to build a role for the line manager which is valuable to the learner, but not essential. If the involvement of a line manager for every learner is essential to the programme, then some learners will be discriminated against – often the very learners who might most benefit from the programme.

We can, of course, consider an alternative to the line manager. Why not use a mentor system instead?

Mentors

In this context, a mentor is someone other than the learner's boss who is charged with advising and counselling the learner, and is drawn into the learning contract process as a third partner.

Where mentors are used – in this context or as part of a more generalized helping relationship – they tend to be senior to the learner, although not necessarily senior in the same line or department (Clutterbuck 1991).

There are strengths and weaknesses in using mentors in the learning contract partnership rather than the learner's boss. On the positive side we might expect the following.

- Mentors will be more sympathetic to a learning/development approach to the learning contract and less project-orientated, simply because they will not have the dual motives of even the best of managers, divided between the desire to develop their subordinates and the need to achieve task objectives through them.

- Mentors should be more sympathetic to a learning/development approach if they have volunteered for the role, or carried it out in the past, or are mentors for several people. This does not reduce the need for clear guidance as to their role in the partnership.
- Mentors are less likely to be too directive or to collude with the learner over the assessment.
- The problems of confidentiality may not arise in the same form as when the third partner is the learner's boss, but much depends on the relationship between the mentor and the boss, and the degree of trust between mentor and learner.

On the negative side, however, we are likely to find less of an ability to:

- cast independent light on the learner's development needs (of course the line manager's opinions on this matter can be sought outside the mentor–learner relationship)
- advise on the realism of the learning contract
- assist the action plan by making learning opportunities available
- assist in assessment through witness testimony or through validating the accuracy of technical information (obviously this testimony can still be sought from the line manager if required).

In composing these lists of advantages and disadvantages, we are dealing with possibilities and likelihoods rather than certainties, because much of the effectiveness of the role depends upon the personalities and skills of the individuals involved.

The strong relationship between the implicit criteria we use to evaluate training and development, and job performance (and its natural assessor, the learner's line manager), means that the line manager will often remain a part of the geometry.

Rather than one triangle – or three-way meeting – there are now four possible three-way discussions of the learner's progress, and potentially six two-way discussions (Figure 12.1).

Even if the boss takes no active part in agreeing the learning contract, and does not discuss the matter at all with mentor or tutor, there will often be a relationship with the learner which adds to the latter's perceptions of what he or she should do, and which includes an assessment by the line manager of the effects of the development programme.

The decision whether to involve line managers or mentors will be made in accordance with the circumstances of each company's case. For the remainder of this chapter we shall refer to the employer's representative as the line manager or the boss of the learner, simply for convenience, while recognizing that much of what is said applies equally well if a mentor is filling the role.

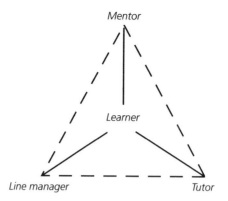

Figure 12.1   The extended learning triangle

Briefing line managers

Certain simple measures can go a long way towards making the most of the contribution the line manager can bring to the learning contract process. In particular, a clear briefing, explaining what is about to happen and the line manager's role in making it happen successfully, can go a long way to avoiding many potential problems.

What is called for is something similar to the priming process for learners, that:

- explains the learning contract approach
- builds motivation and confidence in it
- explains the line manager's role.

Ideally this briefing will take place at about the same time as the learners are being primed. As with the learners, it is more effective to brief the line managers face to face: printed materials might be used to support the briefing, but they will be insufficient in themselves. Experience indicates that learners often have difficulty briefing their line managers effectively (the learners may be struggling to understand the process themselves!) so it is best done by the tutor.

The explanation of the learning contract method will be the same explanation as that provided to the learners, and the same measures should be taken to build confidence in it. The rest of the briefing has a different slant, however, and where possible it is more effective to speak to the line managers separately from the learners, so that they feel better able to ask questions about how the process will relate to them.

It is important to explain and to stress three key features of the learning contract method, in order to try to avoid problems later on.

1.   A learning contract is not the same as a project: it is explicitly about

---

Box 12.3 What is required

Like the learners, the line managers will have certain practical questions about the process. They will want to know:

- the scope of the learning contract: how is the subject chosen? Are there restrictions on the freedom of choice?
- the timing: the scheduling and the size of the learning contract
- assessment: how will the learning contract be assessed? Who will carry out the assessment?

---

     learning and developing skills, not just about doing things, or changing things within the organization.

2.   The payback to the line manager and to the company is not immediate. The learning contract should be relevant to the job and should fit in with current work performance, but line managers should not expect an instant return.

3.   The learning contract works best if the initiative comes from the individual learner and he or she feels responsible for the proposal. The line manager has a role to play in providing help and advice – and some home truths might be called for at times – but, like the tutor, line managers must be careful not to threaten the learner's sense of responsibility for the proposal.

These three points need to be made in a friendly but uncompromising way to indicate that they are fundamental rules, not open to negotiation. It is quite natural for line managers to forget these principles or by their behaviour to ignore them later on, so it is very important for the tutor to set them out clearly at an early stage, so that those who later transgress can be reminded of them.

    As with learners, line managers should be given a clear idea of their role, setting out what is expected of them, how long it will take and when it is scheduled. It is also helpful to stress that the role is quite simple – as opposed to being complex or difficult – and not particularly time-consuming, but of great potential value to the learner. This addresses two common fears experienced by line managers, and provides an additional reason why they should become involved.

Handling problems

The briefing will avoid some of the problems we have discussed in this chapter, but it will not avoid all of them all of the time. As the tutor you will need to cope with them as they arise in the negotiation. The most common concern project proposals and directive line managers.

Project proposals

The line manager puts forward or supports a project. At more junior levels this will frequently involve acquiring or analysing information or establishing a new information system; at more senior levels it may be a substantial change project.

As in cases where the learner puts forward a project proposal, the tutor should look for the learning, or ask the line manager and the learner to look, and remind them of the rule that the learning contract must focus on learning and development, not on creating systems or changing the organization.

If possible, you, as the tutor, may be able to have a chat with the line manager after the three-way discussion, and make enquiries regarding the skills or areas for development they think the learner might consider for future contracts. This may jog the line manager onto the true learning contract path – or it may alert you to the likelihood that all future negotiations will involve a struggle over understanding.

Directive line managers

Where the line manager is obviously directive and puts forward the learning contract proposal, the first action to take is to check the learner's level of acceptance. How does the learner feel about this? This may have only a limited effect, but at least it acknowledges the consent of the learner. The line manager and the learner may have different ideas about what the learner should do, resulting in conflict.

If conflict is apparent in the three-way discussion, as the tutor, you may play a mediating role, helping each party clarify what they propose and exploring underlying reasons for the proposals and the difference of opinion. Such open conflict is not usual. More often the disagreements will have been worked out between the learner and the line manager before the three-way meeting, although sometimes you may be drawn into the dispute by one party or another.

Group support

An effective – although time-consuming – method of supporting learners and line managers who face dilemmas in this area is to set up separate

Box 12.4 A little bit less, a little bit more

Jack, who was Clive's line manager, wanted the contract to be about preparing a set of clear statements on company policy and procedures in respect of certain personnel practices. The policy at the commencement of the contract was to be found in the original legislation and in a variety of union–management agreements and statements by management committees. Jack and Clive worked in the personnel section of one of the company's large departments: whenever a query arose about policy or procedure, Clive had to respond personally. Jack wanted Clive to create a set of guidance notes, written in plain English, explaining policy and procedures in the common problem areas, to reduce the number of queries.

Clive agreed that this would be a sensible measure.

The proposal was, of course, a project; after some discussion the principal learning area (clear written expression) was identified.

Jack wanted Clive to produce guidance notes in twenty different areas by the end of the contract period. These were the main areas Jack had identified as giving rise to queries (at the head of the list, for example, was the procedure for arranging for maternity leave).

The tutor said that production of notes in all twenty areas was not necessary for completion of the learning contract: he suggested a sample of notes from three areas.

The notes themselves, however, would not be sufficient to complete the contract. The tutor suggested some reflection on, and evaluation of, the ways in which Clive had taken the complex statements of his sources and turned them into simple, clear points that the average employee could understand.

Changing the line manager's project proposals into effective learning contracts will often involve this twin process: reducing the output requirement and increasing the amount of other kinds of evidence required to focus attention on learning.

support groups for each, so that learners meet regularly as a group and line managers who are involved in agreeing and assessing contracts also meet on a regular (although probably less frequent) basis.

In a group setting, learners are more likely to be forthcoming about whether they or their manager devised the initial proposal for the learning contract, whether they feel they are really exercising choice, and about what benefits and problems they are experiencing.

Similarly, if a number of line managers are successfully working within the learning contract system as intended, and are seeing positive results from it (which should be the case), then their experiences, shared in discussion, are more likely to have a positive effect on the future behaviour of 'problem' line managers than a one-to-one discussion with a tutor.

Although the meetings are time-consuming, they can be more efficient than attempting to sort out a number of problems on a one-to-one basis.

If this approach is to be used, line managers and learners need to be told about it in good time, and dates fixed for meetings. The atmosphere suffers if the meetings are called hurriedly, for remedial or emergency repair reasons.

Involving a new tutor

In some cases the third partner to the contract may be a tutor: for instance, when the contract is agreed between the learner and their line manager, as part of a staff development process, and the tutor is called in (perhaps from the company's training department) to support the activity. Alternatively, it may occur when the contract tutor wishes to involve a specialist, to apply their expertise to a contract area.

Unless this new party to the contract, the new tutor, is experienced in using learning contracts, they must be thoroughly briefed by the line manager or by the contract tutor, about the use of contracts and about their expected role. Some professional trainers and educators operate in a largely didactic style, and will naturally behave in this way unless they are gently but firmly guided to the contrary. Otherwise they may cling too dogmatically to established blocks of knowledge and traditional sequences of acquiring it, and maintain a mental model of the learning contract as a series of inputs. Learning contracts allow learners and tutors to think in creative and flexible ways about learning and development – but this does not necessarily come easily at first.

In fact, all that we have said about the importance of priming the learner and briefing the line manager applies equally to a new tutor, and similar methods can be used to achieve understanding.

Review

The partnership of the learning triangle can be very effective in establishing and assessing relevant and practical learning contracts. The line manager of the learner has a distinct and valuable role to play. The actual value of the line manager's contribution will depend in part on the attitudes and skills of the particular individual, and in part on the skills of the tutor in providing an adequate and timely briefing and in dealing with any problems as they arise.

References

Argyris, C. and Schon, D. 1978 *Organisational Learning*, Reading, MA: Addison-Wesley.

Ashridge 1996 *360 Degree Feedback – Unguided Missile or Powerful Weapon*, Ashridge Research, UK.

Back, K. and Back, K. 1991 *Assertiveness at Work*, 2nd edn, London: McGraw-Hill.

Barham, K., Fraser, J. and Heath, I. 1988 *Management for the Future*, Ashridge: Foundation for Management Education.

Beaumont, G. 1995 *Review of 100 NVQs and SVQs: A Report to the Department for Education and Employment*, Chesterfield, Derbyshire.

Belbin, R.M. 1981 *Management Teams*, Oxford: Heinemann.

Belbin, R.M. 1993 *Team Roles at Work*, Oxford: Butterworth-Heinemann.

Boak, G. 1991a *Developing Managerial Competences*, London: Pitman.

Boak, G. 1991b 'Three dimensions of personal development', *Industrial and Commercial Training*, **23**(5), pp 21–24.

Boak, G. 1995 'Successful pilot programmes', *Industrial and Commercial Training*, October, **27**(11), pp 9–11.

Boak, G. and Stephenson, M. 1987 'Management learning contracts: from theory to practice', *Journal of European Industrial Training*, **11**(4), pp 4–6, (6), 17–20.

Boyatzis, R. 1982 *The Competent Manager*, New York: Wiley.

Boyatzis, R. 1993 'Beyond competence: the choice to be a leader', *Human Resource Management Review*, **3**(1), pp 1–4.

Brookfield, S.D. 1986 *Understanding and Facilitating Adult Learning*, Milton Keynes: OU.

Caple, T. and Mitchell, L. 1992 *Assessment of Management Competence at Work*, NHS Training Directorate, Bristol.

Casey, D. 1993 'The role of the set adviser', in Pedler, M. (ed.) *Action Learning*, 2nd edn., Aldershot: Gower.

Cheetham, G. 1994 'The developmental effectiveness of the management standards and associated NVQs', Technical Report No 19 for the Employment Department's Learning Methods Branch, March 1994.

Clark, J. 1996 *MA Management Practice: Definitive Document*, The Business School, University of North London.

Clutterbuck, D. 1991 *Everyone Needs a Mentor*, 2nd edn, London: IPM.

Council for Industry and Higher Education 1995 *A Wider Spectrum of Opportunities.*

DfEE 1995 *The National Development Agenda,* Department for Education and Employment.

DfEE 1996 *The National Development Agenda,* Department for Education and Employment.

Edwards, M.R. and Ewen, A.J. 1996 360 *Degree Feedback,* amacom, New York.

Employment Department 1989/90 *Enterprise in Higher Education, Key Features of the EHE Proposals.*

Eraut, M. 1994 *Developing Professional Knowledge and Competence,* London: The Falmer Press.

Eraut, M. and Cole, G. 1993 'Assessment of competence in higher level occupations', *Competence and Assessment,* Issue No 21, Employment Department.

Garavan, T.N. and Sweeney, P. 1994 'Supervisory training and development: the use of learning contracts', *Journal of European Industrial Training,* **18**(2), pp 17–26.

Gattegno, G. 1995 *Work-based Learning for Managers,* 'Teletechy', cited in Karpin 1995.

Hall, J.W. and Kevles, B.L. 1982 *In Opposition to Core Curriculum,* New York: Greenwood Press.

Honey, P. 1989 *Peter Honey's Manual of Management Workshops,* Maidenhead: Peter Honey.

Honey, P. and Mumford, A. 1982 *The Manual of Learning Styles,* Maidenhead: Peter Honey.

Honey, P. and Mumford, A. 1989 *The Manual of Learning Opportunities,* Maidenhead: Peter Honey.

IRS 1993 'Competency and the links to HR practice', Research Report by Human Resource Business Consultants and Industrial Relations Services, London.

Jones, A. and Hendry, C. 1992 'The learning organisation: a review of literature and practice', Centre for Corporate Strategy and Change, Warwick Business School.

Juch, A.H. 1983 *Personal Development,* New York: Wiley.

Kalinauckas, P. and King, H. 1994 *Coaching,* London: IPD.

Kaplan, R.E. 1991 *Beyond Ambition,* San Francisco: Jossey-Bass.

Karpin, D.S. 1995 *Enterprising Nation: Report of the Industry Task Force on Leadership and Management Skills,* Canberra: Australian Government Publishing Service.

Kennedy, G., Benson, J. and McMillan, J. 1984 *Managing Negotiations,* 2nd edn, London: Business Books.

Klemp G.O. Jnr and McClelland, D. 1986 'Executive competence: what characterises intelligent functioning among senior managers?', in Sternberg, R. J. and Wagner, R. K. (eds) *Practical Intelligence: Nature and Origins of Competence in the Everyday World,* Cambridge: Cambridge University Press.

Knowles, M. 1986 *Using Learning Contracts,* San Francisco: Jossey-Bass.

Kolb, D. 1976 *The Learning Style Inventory,* Boston, MA: McBer and Co.

Lawrence, J. 1994 'Action learning – a questioning approach', in Mumford, A. (ed.) *Handbook of Management Development,* Aldershot: Gower.

Laycock, M. and Stephenson, J. (eds) 1993 *Using Learning Contracts in Higher Education,* London: Kogan Page.

Lee, D. (ed.) 1994 *Competence and Assessment,* Compendium No 3, Employment Department, Cambridge: Pendragon Press.

Levy, M. 1991 *Work Based Learning – A Good Practice Model,* Blagdon: Further Education Staff College IB 2845.

Lombardo, M. and Eichinger, R. 1989, 1991 *Tools for developing successful executives*, S. Carolina: Center for Creative Leadership.

Mansfield, B. and Mitchell, L. 1996 *Towards a Competent Workforce*, Aldershot: Gower.

Matthewman, J. 1996 'Annual survey of competency frameworks', *Competency*, **4**(1), Autumn, pp 2–24.

McCall, M.W. Jnr, Lombardo, M.M. and Morrison, A.M. 1988 *The Lessons of Experience: How Successful Executives Develop on the Job*, Lexington, MA: Lexington Books.

MCI 1995 *Senior Management Standards*, London: Management Charter Initiative.

Mitchell, L. 1993 'NVQs/SVQs at higher levels: a discussion paper to the Higher Levels Seminar, October 1992', *Competence and Assessment*, Briefing Series No 8, March 1993, Employment Department.

Mitchell, L. and Bartram, D. 1994 'The place of knowledge and understanding in the development of National Vocational Qualifications and Scottish Vocational Qualifications', *Competence and Assessment*, Briefing Series No 10, October 1994, Employment Department, Cambridge: Pendragon Press.

Mumford, A. 1988 *Developing Top Managers*, Aldershot: Gower.

Mumford, A. 1993 *Management Development: Strategies for Action*, 2nd edn, London: IPM.

NCVQ 1995 *NVQ Criteria and Guidance*, London: National Council for Vocational Qualifications.

Pascoe, K. 1992 'Using management learning contracts in my MBA', Parts I and II, *Executive Development*, **5**(4), **6**(1).

Pedler, M. (ed.) 1997 *Action Learning in Practice*, 3rd edn, Aldershot: Gower.

Pedler, M., Burgoyne, J. and Boydell, T. 1986 *A Manager's Guide to Self Development*, 2nd edn, Maidenhead: McGraw-Hill.

Pedler, M., Burgoyne, J. and Boydell, T. 1991 *The Learning Company*, Maidenhead: McGraw-Hill.

Powers, E. 1987 'Enhancing managerial competence: the American Management Association Competence Programme', *Journal of Management Development*, **6**(4), pp 7–18.

Prideaux, G. and Ford, J.E. 1988 'Management development: competencies, contracts, teams and work-based learning', 1 and 2, *Journal of Management Development*, **7**(1), pp 56–68, (3), pp 12–21.

Rackham, N. and Carlisle, J. 1978 'The effective negotiator', 1 and 2, *Journal of European Industrial Training*, **2**(6), pp 6–10, (7), pp 2–5.

Revans, R. 1980 *Action Learning*, London: Blond and Briggs.

Robinson, B. 1995 'Research and pragmatism in learner support', in Lockwood, F. (ed.) *Open and Distance Learning Today*, London: Routledge.

Rowe, D. 1988 *The Successful Self*, London: Fontana.

Rowntree, D. 1992 *Exploring Open and Distance Learning*, Milton Keynes: Open University.

SCALE 1992 *Learning at Work: the Final Report of the SCALE Project*, Scottish Applications of Learning through Experience, SCOTVEC, Glasgow.

Schon, D. 1983, 1991 *The Reflective Practitioner*, Aldershot: Avebury.

Senge, P. 1991 *The Fifth Discipline: the Art and Practice of the Learning Organisation*, New York: Random House.

Smith, R. 1982 *Learning How to Learn: Applied Theory for Adults*, Milton Keynes: OU.

Spencer, L.M. Jnr and Spencer, S.M. 1993 *Competence at Work*, New York: Wiley.

Stewart-David, W. 1993 'Learning contracts and student placements with employers', in Laycock, M. and Stephenson, J. (eds) *Using Learning Contracts in Higher Education*, London: Kogan Page.

TDLB 1995 *Assessment and Verification Units: National Standards for Training and Development*, Training and Development Lead Body.

Thatcher, M. 1996 'Allowing everyone to have their say', *People Management*, 21 March.

Thompson, D. 1994 'Competent Managers Can be Developed', MA Thesis, University of East London.

Thompson, D. and Stephenson, M. 1991 *Manual of Learning Approaches for Competent Manager Development*, NRMC, Flexible Management Learning Centre, Newcastle Business School, 1995.

Thornton, G.C. and Byham, W.C. 1982 *Assessment Centres and Managerial Performance*, London: Academic Press.

Wolf, A. 1994 'Assessing the broad skills within occupational competence', *Competence and Assessment*, Issue 25, April 1994, Employment Department.

Woodcock, M. and Francis, D. 1996 *The New Unblocked Manager*, Aldershot: Gower.

Index

accrediting learning 5,
  see also qualifications; skill development
Action Learning 16–18, 39, 122, 133, 136
adult learning 6, 39
Argyris, C 9, 136
Ashridge 61
assessment 3–4, 30, 35, 49, 137, 139–52
  criteria 108–110, 140, 142–4, 147–52
  feedback 132, 140, 145
  grading 142
  measures 77, 97–110
  outcomes of 141–2
  on pilot programmes 140–41
  process of 139–41
  see also evidence assessment centres 64–5

Back, K and Back, K 23
Barham, K 9
Beaumont, G 147, 152
Behavioural Event Interview 64–5
Belbin, RM 58–9, 149
Boak, G 15, 56, 141
Boyatzis, R 24, 25, 56, 129, 152
Brookfield, SD 125, 133

Caple, T 147, 152
Casey, D 122
Certificate in Management Studies (CMS)
    15, 18, 31, 33, 130, 157
Cheetham, G 94
Clark, J 3
Clutterbuck, D 160
coaching 123
  see also skills of coaching and counselling
competence and competency 13, 15, 24–7,
    30, 56, 58, 85, 101, 126, 129, 133–4,
    142–3, 18
  see also skills

Council for Industry and Higher Education
    8

Department for Education and Employment
    (DfEE) 8
dependencies 68–70, 78, 113, 117–8
Diploma, postgraduate 15, 38, 143
double loop learning 136

Edwards, MR and Ewen, AJ 61
employer, involvement of 34, 40, 86–7, 94–6,
    131, 153–66
  benefits 153–5
  potential problems of, 156–60
Employment Department 8
Eraut, M 101, 152
  and Cole, G 101
evidence
  authenticity of 148–51, 159
  reliability of 151–2
  validity of 147–8
evidence, forms of
  demonstration 101, 104–6, 148
  interview 101, 104–5, 147–8
  learning log 105, 145
  outcomes 104, 107–8, 148
  portfolio 102
  products, 104, 107–8
  report 101, 104–5, 110, 144–8
  simulation 102, 106, 131
  tape, audio 106
  tape, video 106
  testimony 106–7, 148–50, 155

feedback
  for needs analysis 61–3

Garavan, TN and Sweeney, P 18
Gattegno, G 15

Hall, JW and Kevles, BL 6
Honey, P 18, 59, 89, 145

independent learning 5, 125, 143–4
IRS 24,

Jones, A and Hendry, C 9,
Juch, AH 23

Kalinauckas, P and King, H 123
Kaplan, RE 62
Karpin, DS 24
Kennedy, G 112
Klemp, GO Jnr and McClelland D 65
Knowles, M 6, 39, 44, 109, 148
Kolb, D 18

Lawrence, J 17, 39
Laycock, M and Stephenson, J 6, 93
learning contracts
    benefits 4–6
    characteristics 1, 4, 30
    definition 1, 11, 44
    design 29–35
    drafting the agreement 121–2
    legal status 3
    ownership of 24, 57, 60, 63–4, 70–72, 94–5,
        99–100, 116, 121, 158
    SMART objectives 69
    timing 30–31, 35–9, 49, 91–2, 116–7, 127,
        132, 140
    values associated with use of 33, 39–42,
        126, 144
    for examples of contract topics *see* skills
Learning Cycle 18–20, 22, 44, 89–90, 102–4,
    115, 126, 133, 145–7
learning curve 86
    staged improvement 21–2, 46–7, 115
learning organization 8–9
learning styles 58–9, 89, 133–5
learning triangle 13–14, 41, 153, 156, 161–2,
    166
Lee, D 147, 152
Levy, M 15
Lewin, K 113
lifelong learning 8
Lombardo, M and Eichinger, R

McCall, MW Jnr 15, 90
Management Charter Initiative (MCI) 58
Mansfield, B 8, 24,
Master's degree in Business Administration
    (MBA) 15, 25, 94, 101, 134, 137, 142–3,
    157

Matthewman, J 24
mentor 160–61
Mitchell, L 8, 24, 147, 152
    and Bartram, D 147, 152
motivation of learner 4–5, 24–6, 30, 44–8, 55,
    95, 103, 123, 134
Mumford, Alan 5, 18, 59, 89, 91

National Council for Vocational
    Qualifications (NCVQ) 140, 147, 152
National Vocational Qualification (NVQ) 4,
    10, 15, 97, 101–2, 107, 143
needs analysis 20, 23, 34, 36, 43, 49, 53–66,
    74–6, 84, 86–7, 92–3, 113, 151, 164
    assessment centres 64–5
    feedback 61–3, 132
    self-analysis 53–61, 136
    self-assessment questionnaires 57–61
    training needs analysis 63–64
negotiation
    aims of tutor 68–71
    definition 67
    problems of, 74–80
    process of, 71–4, 112–14
    skills of, 111–24
    three-way 86–7, 94–5, 153–66
Newcastle Business School 15
Northern Regional Management Centre
    (NRMC) 15, 33

ownership of the learning contract 24, 57,
    60, 63–4, 70–72, 94–5, 99–100, 116, 121,
    158

Pascoe, K 15
Pedler, M 9, 17, 145
personal development plan (PDP) 9
placement 10, 93–4
Powers, E 3, 24
preparation 33–4
    priming 33, 38, 43–51, 74–5, 113, 115,
        162–3, 166
    see also needs analysis
Prideaux, G and Ford, JE 18

qualifications 6–8, 10, 37, 40, 86, 97–9, 112,
    137, 142
    see also Certificate in Management Studies;
    Diploma; Master's degree in Business
    Administration; National Vocational
    Qualifications
questionnaires for needs analysis 57–61

Rackham, N and Carlisle, J 114

research projects 53, 73, 109, 126–7, 128, 132, 144
Revans, R 16, 133
Robinson, B 125
Rowe, D 60
Rowntree, D 125

SCALE 8
Scottish Vocational Qualification (SVQ) 4, 143
Schon, D 9, 136, 145
Senge, P 9
skill development 13–17, 18–23, 44–5, 47–50, 75–7, *83–90*, 102–3, 126–37, 142–4, 149
skills
    of appraisal 21, 48, 117
    of assertiveness 21, 98
    of business awareness 48, 150
    of change management 21, 129
    of coaching and counselling 70
    of conceptualization 149
    of computing and information technology (IT) 21, 35, 130
    of company systems, use of, 21, 80, 89
    of financial management 21, 129
    of fluency in foreign languages 80
    of influencing, negotiating and persuading 16, 107, 129
    of interpersonal behaviour 33, 85–7, 105
    of interviewing 21, 69, 101, 105–6, 116
    of leadership 70, 107, 137, 149
    of learning 5, 16, 38
    of logical thinking 129
    of managing meetings 21, 86–7, 106
    of presentation 21, 86–7, 91, 105–6, 109, 132, 148, 151
    of problem solving 129
    of recruitment 48, 69, 106
    of self-confidence 86–8, 119, 129, 149
    of teambuilding and teamworking 16, 47, 85, 101, 119–20
    of time management 21, 89, 95, 98, 101
    of training 21, 70, 93, 107
    of written expression 21, 165
Smith, R 62
Spencer, LM Jnr and Spencer, SM 26
Stephenson, M 15, 17
Stewart-David, W 46
support 34–35, 120, 125–38, 155, 164–6

TDLB 147, 152
Thatcher, M 61
Thompson, D 15, 17, 18, 21, 157
Thornton, GC and Byham WC 64
tutor
    definition 2–3
    role 5–6, 11, 53–5, 68–71, 73–4, 99–101, 115, 118, 133, 137
    skills 74, 114–24

Wolf, A 101, 142, 147
Woodcock, M and Francis, D 58–9
work-based learning 8–11, 34, 40, 44, 54, 73, 131, 148, 154–5
work-based projects 10–11, 90–93, 131, 157–8, 164–5

The Business Approach to Training

Teresa Williams and Adrian Green

The role of the trainer is changing rapidly. Internal trainers are increasingly having to justify their proposed solutions in business terms, while external trainers can sell their services only by helping customers to fulfil their business objectives. In both cases, they need a knowledge of 'business speak' that will enable them to deal with other managers on an equal footing.

At the same time trainers are themselves having to operate in a businesslike way: to recover their costs, to market their services proactively, and so on. This book explains the main ideas governing finance, strategy and marketing. By relating concepts like business planning, cash flow, breakeven analysis, pay back, SWOT analysis and the marketing mix to the training process it removes some of the mystery that surrounds them. The authors use a variety of methods to reinforce the learning, including exercises and activities.

This is a book that bridges the gap between the practice of training and the realities of business. For the trainer determined to survive and flourish in today's demanding climate, it will be invaluable.

Gower

The Complete Guide to People Skills

Sue Bishop

As a manager wanting to get the most out of your team, you need to practise 'people-focused leadership'. You need to encourage your people to contribute fully to the success of your organization, and to do that, you need an armoury of people skills.

Sue Bishop's book provides a comprehensive guide to all of the interpersonal skills that you need to get the best from your team. Skills that you can apply in formal settings, such as recruitment interviews, or appraisals, as well as less formal, such as coaching or counselling. Team skills to help you communicate with, and develop, your people. Skills to handle disciplinary matters, or emotional crises, or to resolve conflict. And skills that you can use when you are just chatting with and enthusing individuals and the team.

*The Complete Guide to People Sk*ills is divided into two parts. Part I gives an overview of the core skills, and offers a brief explanation of some self-development and communication theories.

Part II shows how to apply these skills in different situations. It is arranged alphabetically by topic - from appraisals to teamwork. Each section includes an exercise to help you learn more about the skills and techniques and to apply them in your work.

Gower

Evaluating Management Development, Training and Education

Second Edition

Mark Easterby-Smith

This ambitious book offers a comprehensive guide to evaluation as applied to management development. It deals in detail with the technical aspects of evaluation, but its main value probably lies in its treatment of more subtle and possibly more important questions such as the politics of using evaluations, the range of purposes to which they may be put, and the effect of different contexts on evaluation practice.

The second edition reflects the many changes that have taken place in the world of management since the original text was compiled, in particular the Management Charter Initiative and the move towards competence-based training. The text has been updated throughout, and many new examples and case studies have been added, including a number from Europe and North America. For anyone concerned with management development, whether as teacher, trainer or consultant, Dr Easterby-Smith's text will be indispensable.

Gower

Games for Trainers

3 Volume Set

Andy Kirby

Most trainers use games. And trainers who use games collect new games. Andy Kirby's three-volume compendium contain 75 games in each volume. They range from icebreakers and energizers to substantial exercises in communication. Each game is presented in a standard format which includes summary, statement of objectives, list of materials required, recommended timings and step-by-step instructions for running the event. Photocopiable masters are provided for any materials needed by participants.

All the games are indexed by objectives, and Volume 1 contains an introduction analysing the different kinds of game, setting out the benefits they offer and explaining how to use games to the maximum advantage. It is a programmed text designed to help trainers to develop their own games. Volume 3 reflects current trends in training; in particular the increased attention being paid to stress management and assertiveness. Volumes 2 and 3 contain an integrated index covering all three volumes.

Gower

Gower Handbook of Management Skills

Third Edition

Edited by Dorothy M Stewart

'This is the book I wish I'd had in my desk drawer when I was first a manager. When you need the information, you'll find a chapter to help; no fancy models or useless theories. This is a practical book for real managers, aimed at helping you manage more effectively in the real world of business today. You'll find enough background information, but no overwhelming detail. This is material you can trust. It is tried and tested.'

So writes Dorothy Stewart, describing in the preface the unifying theme behind the new edition of this bestselling *Handbook*. This puts at your disposal the expertise of 25 specialists, each a recognized authority in their particular field. Together, this adds up to an impressive 'one stop library' for the manager determined to make a mark.

Chapters are organised within three parts: Managing Yourself, Managing Other People, and Managing Business. Part I deals with personal skills and includes chapters on self-development and information technology. Part II covers people skills such as listening, influencing and communication. Part III looks at finance, project management, decision-making, negotiating and creativity. A total of 12 chapters are completely new, and the rest have been rigorously updated to fully reflect the rapidly changing world in which we work.

Each chapter focuses on detailed practical guidance, and ends with a checklist of key points and suggestions for further reading.

Gower

How to Measure Training Effectiveness

Third Edition

Leslie Rae

This is a revised and enlarged edition of an outstandingly successful book. In it, Leslie Rae describes a variety of ways in which training can be assessed for effectiveness and value. He covers the entire training process from selecting and planning a training event to validating and testing its outcome. Most of the techniques presented can be applied equally to single events and to a complete programme.

New to the Third Edition:

• Existing material (9 chapters) brought fully up to date
• Three entirely new chapters on the evaluation process added
• Details of the latest competence standards produced by the Training and Development Lead Body.

The book is designed as a practical guide and is written in non-technical language. It will be particularly helpful to newly appointed trainers and to line managers with training responsibility.

Gower

The New Time Manager

Angela V Woodhull

Why is it that, when there are exactly 168 hours in everyone's week, some people accomplish so much more than others? Often they're the same people who appear least stressed and enjoy both personal and professional lives the most.

Dr Woodhull's absorbing book explains the key principles of modern time management and shows how to apply them in our day-to-day activities. Traditional time management revolved mainly around to-do lists and delegating. *The New Time Manager* is concerned far more with factors like developing good working relationships and establishing a healthy lifestyle. For example, New Time Managers:

- prioritize
- communicate effectively
- give constructive feedback
- take time to play
- act to prevent burnout.

The result is a life in balance, with sufficient time for what is important to *you*. Whatever your objective, Dr Woodhull's book, with its practical guidance on every aspect of time, will help you.

Gower